AF449015

God's Words to Women in Ministry

You did not choose Me, but I chose you and appointed you that you should go and bear fruit, and that your fruit should remain, that whatever you ask the Father in My name He may give you.
John 15:16 NKJV

Taiwo Iredele Odubiyi

Also By Taiwo Iredele Odubiyi

Fiction

Pratt Sisters Series
In Love for Us * Tears on My Pillow * To Love Again

Femi and Ibie Series
With This Ring * The Forever Kind of Love

Agape Campus Church Series
You Found Me * Life Goes On * My Desire

Bible Stories
What Changed You? * Too Much of a Good Thing

The Past Series
Shadows from the Past * This Time Around * Then Came You

Baby Miracle Series
Oh Baby! * Sea of Regrets

Redirected Series
Is it Me You're Looking for? * Marriage on Fire

Stand Alone Titles
Love Fever * Love on the Pulpit * My First Love * The One for Me
Shipwrecked With You * When A Man Loves A Woman * I'll Take You There * Never Say Never!

For Children
Rescued by Victor * No One is a Nobody
Greater Tomorrow * The Boy Who Stole
Joe and His Stepmother, Bibi * Nike & the Stranger
Billy the Bully

Nonfiction
30 Things Husbands Do That Hurt Their Wives
30 Things Wives Do That Hurt Their Husbands
Rape & How to Handle it * Devotionals for Singles
God's Words to Singles * God's Words to Couples
God's Words to Older Adults
Real Answers, Real Quick! (for singles)
Real Answers, Real Quick! (for couples)
Divine instructions to live by – 1

Copyright 2021
by Taiwo Iredele Odubiyi

GOD'S WORDS TO WOMEN IN MINISTRY

ISBN: 978-978-979-832-2

Published by:
Tender Heartslink,
Maryland, USA

WhatsApp: +1410-8187482
Website: www.pastortaiwoodubiyi.org
Facebook: Pastor (Mrs.) Taiwo Odubiyi,
              Pastor Taiwo Iredele Odubiyi's Novels & Books,
Twitter: @pastortaiwoodub
Instagram: @pastortaiwoiredeleodubiyi

Editor: TiOluwani Odubiyi
Cover design: TantOluwa Odubiyi

All rights reserved. No part of this publication may be reproduced or transmitted in any form or by any means - electronic, mechanical, photocopying, recording or any other - without the express written permission of the copyright holder or publisher.

A note

Dear fellow Woman in Ministry,

I had started writing the novel ***She Who Finds a Man*** when I felt inspired to write this book to minister to the women in ministry.

This book ***God's Words to Women in Ministry*** has been written to address some of the issues that will be relevant to you as a woman in ministry.

You will find in this book some words of encouragement and several Scriptures, to remind you of God's words, and encourage you to grow in God's grace so that you can finish well and have the expected end - to the glory of God.

Many women, including Pastors' wives ask me questions about ministry, marriage, and life, - how to survive the challenges and fulfill their calling.

In this book, I have shared some of the wisdom gained from God's presence and years of ministry to give you sound wisdom and godly direction. Keep the advice in mind, be a doer of the words of God, and you will find rest for your soul.

As you read the words of this book and reflect on them, I pray they speak to your heart, and that you find joy, encouragement, comfort, and fulfilment, in Jesus name.

I also pray for you that ***our God would count you worthy of this calling, and fulfill all the good pleasure of His goodness and the work of faith with power, that the name of our Lord Jesus Christ may be glorified in you, and you in Him, according to the grace of our God and the Lord Jesus Christ. (II Thessalonians 1:11-12)***

Pastor Taiwo Iredele Odubiyi
It's All About You, Jesus!

Contents

Page

About ...

When ...

God's Words to Women in Ministry

About Being an exemplary leader

*A good name is to be chosen rather than great riches, Loving
favour rather than silver and gold.
Proverbs 22:1 NKJV*

*You are the salt of the earth; but if the salt loses its flavour,
how shall it be seasoned? It is then good for nothing but to be
thrown out and trampled underfoot by men.
Matthew 5:13 NKJV*

*Let your light so shine before men, that they may see your
good works and glorify your Father in heaven.
Matthew 5:16 NKJV*

*Then Jesus spoke to the multitudes and to His disciples,
saying:
The scribes and the Pharisees sit in Moses' seat. Therefore
whatever they tell you to observe,
that observe and do, but do not do according to their works;
for they say, and do not do.
Matthew 23:1-3 NKJV*

For I have given you an example, that you should do as I have done to you.
John 13:15 NKJV

But beware lest somehow this liberty of yours become a stumbling block to those who are weak.
For if anyone sees you who have knowledge eating in an idol's temple, will not the conscience of him who is weak be emboldened to eat those things offered to idols?
I Corinthians 8:9-10 NKJV

Imitate me, just as I also imitate Christ.
I Corinthians 11:1 NKJV

in all things showing yourself to be a pattern of good works; in doctrine showing integrity, reverence, incorruptibility, sound speech that cannot be condemned,
that one who is an opponent may be ashamed, having nothing evil to say of you.
Titus 2:7-8 NKJV

having your conduct honourable among the Gentiles, that when they speak against you as evildoers, they may, by your good works which they observe, glorify God in the day of visitation.
I Peter 2:12 NKJV

For to this you were called, because Christ also suffered for us, leaving us an example, that you should follow His steps:
I Peter 2:21 NKJV

Words of encouragement

In the novel *The Forever Kind of Love*, I wrote:

The General Overseer. added, "That is why I'm bringing it up, to caution you and teach you how to resist and overcome this evil. Sadly, quite a number of men of God have sabotaged their ministries by sexual sins. I've had to counsel more than two men of God who fell into adultery ... but may I tell you the truth? There's really no reason for a man of God to fall into sexual sin or have a sex scandal over his head. It happens because people ignore the words of God and become very careless."

Some of the people nodded in agreement.

The G.O. spoke again. "I have been in the ministry for over thirty two years and I have never had the issue of sex scandal. Never!"

He paused for effect, and then went on. "Am I saying that I'm perfect? No. It has been by God's grace. There are things God has taught me, which I do, and have helped me to stay away from sex scandals. These are the things I want to share with you this morning."

In this novel, the General Overseer was being a good example to his ministers and others around him by living a sex scandal free life, and teaching them how to achieve it.

As a woman in ministry, you should be an example of a believer, not only to the people you're leading but to all around you which include your family members, children, friends, staff, believers, and unbelievers. You need to realise that you're surrounded by a cloud of witnesses. People, including unbelievers are watching you.

Seeing then that you are surrounded by so great a cloud of witnesses, you should lay aside every weight, and the sin which can easily ensnare you, and run with endurance the race that is set before you.
Hebrews 12:1

Being a good example does not mean you are perfect; mistakes can happen because only God is perfect. However, because you have the Spirit of God in you, you don't have to make a mistake or sin, but if you do, you should correct yourself and make sure the same mistake is not repeated.

My little children, these things I write to you, so that you may not sin. And if anyone sins, we have an Advocate with the Father, Jesus Christ the righteous.
I John 2:1 NKJV

Be strong in the Lord and do things the right way - that is what being a good example is all about.

The manner of life that God expects from those who profess to be Christians is what He expects from the ministers of the gospel. He doesn't have a different set of rules for ministers. Women in Ministry should live holy for God is holy.

but as He who called you is holy, you also be holy in all your conduct, because it is written, "Be holy, for I am holy."
I Peter 1:15-16 NKJV

As a woman in ministry, people should be able to follow your example while you're following the example of Jesus. You should be able to say what Paul said in ***1Corinthians 11:1, "Imitate me, just as I also imitate Christ."***

And so, don't just talk about the gospel, live it!

To be a good example, you need to fix your eyes on Jesus.

Looking unto Jesus, the author and finisher of our faith, who for the joy that was set before Him endured the cross, despising the shame, and has sat down at the right hand of the throne of God.
Hebrews 12:2 NKJV

Also, continue to walk with God and be led by the Holy Spirit, for without God you can do nothing, but with God all things are possible.

Another thing that will help you is to imitate those who are truly following God, for those who walk with the wise shall be wise.

As I wrote in the book *Divine Instructions to live by*, to imitate is to behave in a similar way to someone or copy or mimic. Several Scriptures encourage us to be around and imitate godly people. This is because we often become like the people we are around.

And we desire that each one of you show the same diligence to the full assurance of hope until the end, that you do not become sluggish, but imitate those who through faith and patience inherit the promises.
Hebrews 6:11-12 NKJV

Paul instructed the disciples of Jesus to imitate him and other true followers of Jesus.

Brethren, join in following my example, and note those who so walk, as you have us for a pattern.
Philippians 3:17 NKJV

By being a good example, you may lead some people to Christ. It will also make them want to imitate you, which will make them live right, and this will bring glory to God.

Being a good example is about how you live. If a leader lives in sin or acts in a manner that is improper, it causes confusion in the hearts of the people being led which can make them fall.

Paul instructed Timothy to set a pattern for the believers in some ways.

Let no one look down on [you because of] your youth, but be an example and set a pattern for the believers in speech, in conduct, in love, in faith, and in [moral] purity.
1 Timothy 4:12 AMP

As a woman in ministry, you should be an example in your words, conduct, love for people, faith in God, and moral purity.

You should also learn to apologise when wrong. Don't be proud, be honest, be truthful, faithful, dependable, a promise keeper, and a good follower of the Lord Jesus.

Also, in ministry, show seriousness and an excellent spirit.

And in all things show yourself to be an example of good works, with purity in doctrine, having the strictest regard for integrity and truth, dignified, sound and beyond reproach in instruction, so that the opponent of the faith will be shamed, having nothing bad to say about you.
Titus 2:7-8 AMP

Be a good and godly example.

God's Words to Women in Ministry

About Choosing whom to marry
– if unmarried

Nor shall you make marriages with them. You shall not give your daughter to their son, nor take their daughter for your son.
For they will turn your sons away from following Me, to serve other gods; so the anger of the LORD will be aroused against you and destroy you suddenly.
Deuteronomy 7:3,4

I will instruct you and teach you in the way you should go; I will guide you with My eye.
Psalm 32:8

Delight yourself also in the LORD, and He shall give you the desires of your heart.
Psalm 37:4

I will set nothing wicked before my eyes; I hate the work of those who fall away; it shall not cling to me.

A perverse heart shall depart from me; I will not know wickedness.
Psalm 101:3,4

My eyes shall be on the faithful of the land, that they may dwell with me; he who walks in a perfect way, he shall serve me.
Psalm 101:6

Trust in the LORD with all your heart, and lean not on your own understanding.
Proverbs 3:5NKJV

There is a way that seems right to a man, but its end is the way of death.
Proverbs 14:12 NKJV

Do not be unequally yoked together with unbelievers. For what fellowship has righteousness with lawlessness? And what communion has light with darkness?
And what accord has Christ with Belial? Or what part has a believer with an unbeliever?
2Corinthians 6:14,15 NKJV

Words of encouragement

In the novel *With This Ring*, I wrote: *Men still approached Pastor Ibie for a relationship but she had not found a man worth having among them. Presently, a director of the company she worked with, a French man had been showing interest in her. He would like to marry her but she had told him she was not interested because they were not of the same faith. She would not compromise her walk with God just to get married. That would be a recipe for disaster. She needed a certain type of man: good and godly.*

The Bible makes us know that there is a way that seems right to a man, but its end is the way of death. Choosing the wrong person could be very costly as it could affect the decision-maker's destiny, ministry, and life.

Being a Christian and a woman in ministry, you should not consider a non-Christian man for marriage, no matter the status of the person or how nice he appears to be. You should not marry just any man. God's word is very clear about this.

Do not be unequally yoked together with unbelievers. For what fellowship has righteousness with lawlessness? And what communion has light with darkness?

And what accord has Christ with Belial? Or what part has a believer with an unbeliever?
2Corinthians 6:14,15 NKJV

In addition, you shouldn't marry a man solely because he claims to be a Christian. As a woman in ministry, you should trust God to give you a man who loves the Lord and who will understand your calling.

In the novel *Love on the Pulpit,* Teni asked Dave, "Will it be alright to ask what it is you're looking for in a woman?"

He answered, "Simply put, maturity and stability, in all ways spiritually, emotionally and physically. She must also understand my calling and accept it."

Therefore, the process leading to the choice of partner must be taken seriously. For believers, marriage is a life-long contract, therefore in choosing a life partner, you must ask yourself, "Is this person worth spending the rest of my life with? Are we compatible? Is he the will of God for me? What is God saying?"

One of the things that will help in making a good choice and honoring God is to know and be convinced about your purpose in life. Without clarity on your purpose, you might end up making a mistake in choosing the wrong partner- a partner who might derail you from your purpose. If you are unsure or unclear about God's purpose for you, now, more than ever, is the time to seek God's vision for your life.

Only by this revelation can you gain insight on whom a suitable life partner would be for you

Furthermore, you need to have knowledge of who the right man is.

As in everything, let God let God guide you when it comes to choosing a life partner.

God's Words to Women in Ministry

About Clothes, Appearance

Forty years You sustained them in the wilderness; They lacked nothing; Their clothes did not wear out And their feet did not swell.
Nehemiah 9:21 NKJV

She makes tapestry for herself; Her clothing is fine linen and purple.
Strength and honour are her clothing; She shall rejoice in time to come.
Proverbs 31:22, 25 NKJV

"Therefore I say to you, do not worry about your life, what you will eat or what you will drink; nor about your body, what you will put on. Is not life more than food and the body more than clothing?
Look at the birds of the air, for they neither sow nor reap nor gather into barns; yet your heavenly Father feeds them. Are you not of more value than they?
Which of you by worrying can add one cubit to his stature?

"So why do you worry about clothing? Consider the lilies of the field, how they grow: they neither toil nor spin; and yet I say to you that even Solomon in all his glory was not arrayed like one of these.
Now if God so clothes the grass of the field, which today is, and tomorrow is thrown into the oven, will He not much more clothe you, O you of little faith?
"Therefore, do not worry, saying, 'What shall we eat?' or 'What shall we drink?' or 'What shall we wear?'
For after all these things the Gentiles seek. For your heavenly Father knows that you need all these things.
But seek first the kingdom of God and His righteousness, and all these things shall be added to you.
Matthew 6:25-33 NKJV

that you put off, concerning your former conduct, the old man which grows corrupt according to the deceitful lusts, and be renewed in the spirit of your mind,
and that you put on the new man which was created according to God, in true righteousness and holiness.
Ephesians 4:22-24 NKJV

Therefore, as the elect of God, holy and beloved, put on tender mercies, kindness, humility, meekness, longsuffering;
Colossians 3:12 NKJV

in like manner also, that the women adorn themselves in modest apparel, with propriety and moderation,

*not with braided hair or gold or pearls or costly clothing,
but, which is proper for women professing godliness, with
good works.*
I Timothy 2:9-10 NKJV

*Do not let your adornment be merely outward—arranging
the hair, wearing gold, or putting on fine apparel—
rather let it be the hidden person of the heart, with the
incorruptible beauty of a gentle and quiet spirit, which is
very precious in the sight of God.*
I Peter 3:3-4 NKJV

Words of encouragement

As a woman in ministry, you should not forget that you're representing God, and you need to represent Him well, even in your dressing.

I sometimes hear people say, "This is what I like to wear," but as a woman in ministry, it should not be so much about what you like, but about what the One Who has called you (God) likes and wants you to do.

If you have been crucified with Christ; then it should no longer be you who lives, but Christ living in you; and the life which you now live in the flesh you should live by faith in the Son of God, who loved you and gave Himself for you. *(Galatians 2:20)*

You also need to know that as a leader, some people will see you as a role model and want to follow your example. Be a good example to them even in your dressing. Let them know how to dress with dignity and strength like the virtuous woman in *Proverbs 31*.

You don't have to wear expensive clothes, but if you have expensive clothes or can afford them, feel free to wear them. Enjoy the blessings of God and glorify Him in your dressing. However, expensive clothes are not a requirement to being in ministry.

And it is not essential to have surplus of clothes and clothing items, but if you do have them, wear them, and give glory to God for the provision of those items.

On the other hand, you should not be shabbily or carelessly dressed. If you are unable to afford expensive clothes, you should still look presentable. Let your clothes be clean, ironed, and in good condition. Your shoes, hair, etc should also be appropriate.

Another thing to know is that God watches over His own, and takes good care of them. He provides for His children as Jesus pointed out in *Matthew 6.*

Now if God so clothes the grass of the field, which today is, and tomorrow is thrown into the oven, will He not much more clothe you, O you of little faith?

The clothes and shoes that you have may be cheap, however, don't let your heart be troubled. What really matters is that they are neat and in good condition. Be sure they are not torn. Wear them, carry yourself well, and do what God has called you to do. As you faithfully continue to serve God, He will provide for you, and your needs will be met.

If you do need more clothes, learn to sow clothes into other people's lives and you'll be amazed at how God will cause your need to be met. This works and it is because it's a biblical principle. It works not only in the area of clothes, but in other areas too, such as finance.

Give, and it will be given to you: good measure, pressed down, shaken together, and running over will be put into your bosom. For with the same measure that you use, it will be measured back to you.
Luke 6:38 NKJV

It's good to look good and presentable, but don't let your confidence rest in your possessions or ability to afford designer clothes or the money that you have. Your confidence must be in God Who has given you life and Who has called you into the ministry. Let him that boasts boast that he knows God.

Command those who are rich in this present age not to be haughty, nor to trust in uncertain riches but in the living God, who gives us richly all things to enjoy. I Timothy 6:17 NKJV

Don't focus too much on your appearance and keeping up with what is trending. Don't try to conform to the world as the Bible warns in Romans 12.

And do not be conformed to this world, but be transformed by the renewing of your mind, that you may prove what is that good and acceptable and perfect will of God.
Romans 12:2 NKJV

Rather, you should put on the Lord Jesus and make no provision for the flesh, to gratify its desires.
Romans 13:14

Fashion and other things will change but the will and the word of God will not change.

Dress appropriately as befits a woman in ministry who is surrendered to Jesus.

Your appearance says a lot about you! Some clothes are not appropriate for your calling as they reveal too much and take away from your message/calling. Avoid wearing outfits that glorify your flesh and divert attention away from Christ. Remember, most people are labelled based on their appearance. What lasting impressions do you want your appearance to leave with people?

A woman with an ulterior motive meets him. She is dressed as a prostitute.
Proverbs 7:10 GW

Do not dress in a shabby manner. If you appear raggedy or scruffy, people might be discouraged from receiving the word you have for them.

Ministry is about people– letting the glory of God radiate through you to draw people close to God. Jesus shed His blood for the church, and so you need to be led by God to know what He wants, even in this area.

Your dressing should bring respect to you and glory to God.

Therefore, whether you eat or drink, or whatever you do, do all to the glory of God.
I Corinthians 10:31 NKJV

Moderation must be your watchword. The Lord is at hand.

God's Words to Women in Ministry

About Discouragement and hurt

The Lord will fight for you, and you shall hold your peace.
Exodus 14:14 NKJV

Then Saul said, "I have sinned. Return, my son David. For I will harm you no more, because my life was precious in your eyes this day. Indeed I have played the fool and erred exceedingly."
And David answered and said, "Here is the king's spear. Let one of the young men come over and get it.
May the Lord repay every man for his righteousness and his faithfulness; for the Lord delivered you into my hand today, but I would not stretch out my hand against the Lord 's anointed.
And indeed, as your life was valued much this day in my eyes, so let my life be valued much in the eyes of the Lord, and let Him deliver me out of all tribulation."
I Samuel 26:21-24 NKJV

Come to Me, all you who labor and are heavy laden, and I will give you rest.
Take My yoke upon you and learn from Me, for I am gentle and lowly in heart, and you will find rest for your souls.
Matthew 11:28-29 NKJV

Then Peter came to Him and said, "Lord, how often shall my brother sin against me, and I forgive him? Up to seven times?"
Jesus said to him, "I do not say to you, up to seven times, but up to seventy times seven.
Matthew 18:21-22 NKJV

Beloved, do not avenge yourselves, but rather give place to wrath; for it is written, "Vengeance is Mine, I will repay," says the Lord.
Therefore "If your enemy is hungry, feed him; If he is thirsty, give him a drink; For in so doing you will heap coals of fire on his head."
Do not be overcome by evil, but overcome evil with good.
Romans 12:19-21 NKJV

Now whom you forgive anything, I also forgive. For if indeed I have forgiven anything, I have forgiven that one for your sakes in the presence of Christ, lest Satan should take advantage of us; for we are not ignorant of his devices.
II Corinthians 2:10-11 NKJV

Let all bitterness, wrath, anger, clamor, and evil speaking be put away from you, with all malice. And be kind to one another, tenderhearted, forgiving one another, even as God in Christ forgave you.
Ephesians 4:31-32 NKJV

bearing with one another, and forgiving one another, if anyone has a complaint against another; even as Christ forgave you, so you also must do.
But above all these things put on love, which is the bond of perfection.
And let the peace of God rule in your hearts, to which also you were called in one body; and be thankful.
Colossians 3:13-15 NKJV

Pursue peace with all people, and holiness, without which no one will see the Lord: looking carefully lest anyone fall short of the grace of God;
lest any root of bitterness springing up cause trouble, and by this many become defiled;
Hebrews 12:14-15 NKJV

But He gives more grace. Therefore He says: "God resists the proud, But gives grace to the humble."
Therefore submit to God. Resist the devil and he will flee from you.
James 4:6-7 NKJV

Words of encouragement

In ministry and life, discouragement and hurt will come, and it's not a matter of if, but when and who it will come through. Be prepared, don't let satan spring a surprise on you.

The offenses that will hurt most are the ones from the people you trust or those you have invested so much in, spiritually and financially.

When it happens however, don't allow yourself to be discouraged and don't think of quitting ministry. Rather, put your trust in God and forgive whoever has hurt you just as Jesus forgave the people who were nailing Him to the cross.

Then Jesus said, "Father, forgive them, for they do not know what they do." And they divided His garments and cast lots.
Luke 23:34 NKJV

Of course it's not easy to forget hurt and betrayal, but you need to remember that your fight is ***not against flesh and blood but against principalities and powers, against the rulers of the darkness of this world, against spiritual wickedness in high places. Ephesians 6:12 NKJV***

Satan will use every means possible to try to stop you from setting his captives free. He will use people's actions and words to hurt and discourage you. He might even try to use your spouse, children, and other family members to stop you. Don't forget - it's a spiritual warfare.

Whenever you experience this, look beyond what you can see, and realise that satan is the one behind it. Don't be ignorant of his devises. *(2Corinthians 2:11)*

Don't allow satan to derail or stop you. Be strong in the Lord and in the power of His might.

At a time like this, remind yourself of the words of God and confess them. Here is another Scripture:

You are of God, little children, and have overcome them, because He who is in you is greater than he who is in the world. They are of the world. Therefore, they speak as of the world, and the world hears them. We are of God. He who knows God hears us; he who is not of God does not hear us. By this we know the spirit of truth and the spirit of error.
I John 4:4-6 NKJV

In addition, remind yourself of the fact that those people did not call you into the ministry, God did. Your calling was born, not of blood, nor of the will of the flesh, nor of the will of man, but of God. *(John 1:13 NKJV)*

They did not choose you, but God chose you and appointed you that you should go and bear fruit for Him and that your fruit should abide, so that whatever you ask Him in Jesus' name, He may give it to you. *(Ephesians 15:16)*

When you've been hurt, spend some time with God, pour your heart out to Him, and let Him know how you feel. Ask Him to help you and He will strengthen you. Your strength and heart will be renewed, and you will feel better.

This reminds me of the song:

Lord, You know I need a brand new touch,
My strength of yesterday is gone,
If You give me Lord, a brand new touch,
I'll have the strength to carry on.

Get rid of hurt, bitterness, etc, and continue walking in love, doing what is right. This is not easy to do, I must admit. The last thing you want to do is forgive the people who hurt you, you want your pound of flesh. You should yield to the Spirit of God however and forgive.

In my novel *In Love For Us*, Ben experienced betrayal and hurt, and he thought of getting even.

I wrote in the novel:

For a while, he concentrated on the TV, following the documentary program being shown, but not for long. In fact, he didn't realize his thoughts had drifted back to Tolu immediately until a voice in the TV brought him back to the present.

He still had not decided if he should employ her even though he had prayed and asked God to tell him what to do. He knew he was still bitter and resentful and that was unbecoming of a Christian. He remembered a sermon he had heard preached on disappointments. Yes, he was disappointed and it still hurt but he learnt from that sermon that if a disappointment was not handled the right way, it could lead to bitterness and unforgiveness, and the person could end up destroying himself.

The bitterness and pain felt strange to him. He had thought nobody, and nothing could hurt him or make him get disturbed but what he was experiencing now shocked him. ...

His mind went back to that moment six years ago. Her mother in particular had been very insulting, telling him to stay away from Tolu as ... he was not her idea of a son-in-law. She had said a lot of things to him that he still remembered. ...

... He kept sending messages to Tolu, and twice, he sent friends to discuss with her but there was never a reply from her and eventually, he stopped getting in touch. He stayed away, disappointed and shattered.

Something told him he should employ her as Yvonne had said and not think too much of it but on the other hand, he didn't want to, if only to prove a point to her and her mother that he had made it after all. He wanted his own pound of flesh.

Ben sipped his tea as he thought of taking his pound of flesh. Gently, a voice spoke to him to trust in the Lord with all his heart and not lean on his own understanding. He heaved a heavy sigh and shook his head. Well, he guessed he must do the right thing. And if he was to employ her, he might as well do it without further delay. There was no point in hanging about, he decided, but he would keep her at an arm's length.

Bringing out Tolu's C.V. from where he had put it two weeks ago, he wrote her name and address on an envelope and called his secretary.

(Excerpts from the novel *In Love For Us*)

Furthermore, ask the Holy Spirit for the spirit of discernment so that you may know how to handle everyone you encounter in the ministry. Some people may be in your life for a season or for a purpose. Only God can reveal this to you. People are not perfect and so don't expect perfection from them. Some of them are hurting and might hurt you intentionally or unintentionally.

Put your trust in God, apply wisdom, pray for them, forgive them, keep on loving them, and remain in your calling.

Don't quit.

God's Words to Women in Ministry

About Envy

A sound heart is life to the body, But envy is rottenness to the bones.
Proverbs 14:30 NKJV

And even as they did not like to retain God in their knowledge, God gave them over to a debased mind, to do those things which are not fitting;
being filled with all unrighteousness, sexual immorality, wickedness, covetousness, maliciousness;
full of envy, murder, strife, deceit, evil-mindedness; they are whisperers, backbiters, haters of God,
violent, proud, boasters, inventors of evil things, disobedient to parents, undiscerning, untrustworthy, unloving, unforgiving, unmerciful;
who, knowing the righteous judgment of God, that those who practice such things are deserving of death, not only do the same but also approve of those who practice them.
Romans 1:28-32 NKJV

for you are still carnal. For where there are envy, strife, and divisions among you, are you not carnal and behaving like mere men?
I Corinthians 3:3 NKJV

Love suffers long and is kind; love does not envy; love does not parade itself, is not puffed up;
I Corinthians 13:4 NKJV

Let nothing be done through selfish ambition or conceit, but in lowliness of mind let each esteem others better than himself.
Philippians 2:3 NKJV

But if you have bitter envy and self-seeking in your hearts, do not boast and lie against the truth.
This wisdom does not descend from above, but is earthly, sensual, demonic.
For where envy and self-seeking exist, confusion and every evil thing are there.
James 3:14-16 NKJV

Therefore submit to God. Resist the devil and he will flee from you.
James 4:7 NKJV

Therefore, laying aside all malice, all deceit, hypocrisy, envy, and all evil speaking, as newborn babes, desire the pure milk of the word, that you may grow thereby, if indeed you have tasted that the Lord is gracious.
I Peter 2:1-3 NKJV

Words of encouragement

Envy is one of the things you will need to stay away from if you want to please God and do ministry right without derailing or stumbling.

Envy is to have bad feelings or resentment towards a person because of what the person possesses which you seem to lack.

It is born out of comparison, and the Bible says that those who compare themselves with themselves are not wise.

For we dare not class ourselves or compare ourselves with those who commend themselves. But they, measuring themselves by themselves, and comparing themselves among themselves, are not wise.
II Corinthians 10:12 NKJV

Envy leads to selfish ambitions which in turn will make a person begin to do or say things that are not right. Out of envy, some people have stepped into another person's calling or ministry which God did not call them into. It can cause loss of focus in ministry.

Envy is clearly of the devil and as I like to say, behind every evil is the devil.

Envy makes a person forget what he or she has, what God has done, and can do. The person becomes dissatisfied and longs for what he or she doesn't have yet.
If you realise that you're becoming envious of others or someone in particular, pray against it that you may overcome it. There's nothing you cannot pray about for with God all things are possible.

And if you see this vice in a friend in ministry, prayerfully encourage the person to shun it. But if the person is not willing to change or is a bad influence on you, you may need to separate yourself or keep the person at an arm's length without hating the person.

The Bible reveals in *Galatians 5* that those who practise envy and other works of the flesh will not make heaven.

Now the works of the flesh are evident, which are: adultery, fornication, uncleanness, lewdness, idolatry, sorcery, hatred, contentions, jealousies, outbursts of wrath, selfish ambitions, dissensions, heresies, envy, murders, drunkenness, revelries, and the like; of which I tell you beforehand, just as I also told you in time past, that those who practice such things will not inherit the kingdom of God.
Galatians 5:19-21 NKJV

In the Bible, Rachel envied her sister, Leah because Leah had children.

Now when Rachel saw that she bore Jacob no children, Rachel envied her sister, and said to Jacob, "Give me children, or else I die!"
Genesis 30:1 NKJV

And because King Saul envied David, he decided to kill David. The Spirit of God left him and an evil spirit took over.

So the women sang as they danced, and said: "Saul has slain his thousands, And David his ten thousands."
Then Saul was very angry, and the saying displeased him; and he said, "They have ascribed to David ten thousands, and to me they have ascribed only thousands. Now what more can he have but the kingdom?"
So Saul eyed David from that day forward.
I Samuel 18:7-9 NKJV

I wrote about Saul and David in the novel *What Changed You?*. The following are excerpts.

The next day, Saul was feeling greatly distressed and angry. As he sat, he had a spear in his hand. He had not been the same since the women who came to welcome the army of Israel sang and gave David more recognition.

David was summoned and he came to stand before Saul. When Saul saw him, he began to shout and curse. Some of the servants moved back to stand by the door.

Jonathan was not present. David looked at Abner and Abner told him, "Go ahead."

He began to play music. After some time, the King became quiet.

David looked at him and saw that he looked a little calm, with his eyes closed.

Suddenly, Saul began to prophesy, talking about the greatness of God and His plans for the children of Israel.

David was happy that the King was feeling better. He continued singing and playing the harp.

Saul continued to prophesy. Then he began to say that God had chosen David to be king over His people, Israel.

Shocked, David stared at the King. Then he glanced around and saw surprise on the faces of the men present.

Saul went on, blessing David.

David was still looking at Saul as he continued to play music.

Then, as suddenly as Saul started to prophesy, he stopped and opened his eyes, breathing hard. He glanced around at the men until his eyes came to David. The eyes that met David's were full of anger.

David was confused. Hadn't the King just prophesied? He lowered his eyes and continued to sing and play the harp.

Suddenly, Saul threw his spear at David to pin him to the wall, but David moved away just in time. All the men also ducked in fear.

Terrified, David ran out from the palace.

In ministry, you will come across different people with different graces.

Our bodies have many parts, but these parts don't all do the same thing. In the same way, even though we are many individuals, Christ makes us one body and individuals who are connected to each other. God in His kindness gave each of us different gifts ... (**Romans 12:4-6 GW**)

Here are the things you should do:

Pray against envy.

Therefore submit to God. Resist the devil and he will flee from you.
James 4:7 NKJV

Focus on what God has called you to do.

But as God has distributed to each one, as the Lord has called each one, so let him walk. And so I ordain in all the churches.
I Corinthians 7:17 NKJV

Put your trust in God.

Trust in the Lord with all your heart, And lean not on your own understanding; In all your ways acknowledge Him, And He shall direct your paths. Proverbs 3:5-6 NKJV

Be satisfied with what you have.

Let your conduct be without covetousness; be content with such things as you have. For He Himself has said, "I will never leave you nor forsake you." Hebrews 13:5 NKJV

Don't let your emotions rule you.

God's Words to Women in Ministry

About Excellence in ministry

Do you see a man who excels in his work? He will stand before kings; He will not stand before unknown men. Proverbs 22:29 NKJV

She also rises while it is yet night, And provides food for her household, And a portion for her maidservants.
She girds herself with strength, And strengthens her arms.
She perceives that her merchandise is good, And her lamp does not go out by night.
She makes tapestry for herself; Her clothing is fine linen and purple.
Strength and honor are her clothing; She shall rejoice in time to come.
She opens her mouth with wisdom, And on her tongue is the law of kindness.
She watches over the ways of her household, And does not eat the bread of idleness.
Her children rise up and call her blessed; Her husband also, and he praises her:

"Many daughters have done well, But you excel them all."
Proverbs 31:15, 17-18, 22, 25-29 NKJV

Then this Daniel distinguished himself above the governors and satraps, because an excellent spirit was in him; and the king gave thought to setting him over the whole realm.
Daniel 6:3 NKJV

Then they went into Capernaum, and immediately on the Sabbath He entered the synagogue and taught. And they were astonished at His teaching, for He taught them as one having authority, and not as the scribes.
Mark 1:21-22 NKJV

But as you abound in everything—in faith, in speech, in knowledge, in all diligence, and in your love for us— see that you abound in this grace also.
II Corinthians 8:7 NKJV

And whatever you do, do it heartily, as to the Lord and not to men,
knowing that from the Lord you will receive the reward of the inheritance; for you serve the Lord Christ.
Colossians 3:23-24 NKJV

Study and do your best to present yourself to God approved, a workman [tested by trial] who has no reason to be ashamed, accurately handling and skillfully teaching the word of truth. But avoid all irreverent babble

and godless chatter [with its profane, empty words], for it will lead to further ungodliness,
2 Timothy 2:15-16 AMP

having your conduct honorable among the Gentiles, that when they speak against you as evildoers, they may, by your good works which they observe, glorify God in the day of visitation.
in all things showing yourself to be a pattern of good works; in doctrine showing integrity, reverence, incorruptibility, sound speech that cannot be condemned, that one who is an opponent may be ashamed, having nothing evil to say of you.
Titus 2:7-8 NKJV

But now He has obtained a more excellent ministry, inasmuch as He is also Mediator of a better covenant, which was established on better promises.
Hebrews 8:6 NKJV

But also for this very reason, giving all diligence, add to your faith virtue, to virtue knowledge, to knowledge self-control, to self-control perseverance, to perseverance godliness, to godliness brotherly kindness, and to brotherly kindness love. For if these things are yours and abound, you will be neither barren nor unfruitful in the knowledge of our Lord Jesus Christ.
II Peter 1:5-8 NKJV

Words of encouragement

The Bible says a lot about the Excellency of God and His excellent name.

O Lord, our Lord, How excellent is Your name in all the earth, Who have set Your glory above the heavens!
Psalms 8:1 NKJV

The Bible also says that God is perfect and those who worship Him must work toward perfection.

Therefore you shall be perfect, just as your Father in heaven is perfect.
Matthew 5:48 NKJV

It is a privilege to be called and used by God, therefore we must do it well with an excellent spirit. Mediocrity or laziness should not be tolerated in ministry.

The Psalmist said, *"God is the King of the whole earth. Make your best music for Him!" (Psalms 47:7 GW)*

Another version of the Bible says – Play skillfully, to His glory!

If you're into music, sing well. If you preach, preach well. As a teacher of the Word, teach well. Whatever God has called you to do, do it and do it well to the glory of God!

A woman in ministry should study and do her best to present herself to God approved, a workman tested by trial who has no reason to be ashamed, accurately handling and skillfully teaching the word of truth. She should avoid all irreverent babble and godless chatter, with its profane, empty words, for it will lead to further ungodliness. *(2 Timothy 2:15-16 AMP)*

God in His kindness gave each of us different gifts. If your gift is speaking what God has revealed, make sure what you say agrees with the Christian faith. If your gift is serving, then devote yourself to serving. If it is teaching, devote yourself to teaching. If it is encouraging others, devote yourself to giving encouragement. If it is sharing, be generous. If it is leadership, lead enthusiastically. If it is helping people in need, help them cheerfully.
Romans 12:6-8 GW

In ministry, show seriousness, and be an example of good works, with purity in doctrine, having the strictest regard for integrity and truth, dignified, sound and beyond reproach in instruction, so that the opponent of the faith will be shamed, having nothing bad to say about you. *(Titus 2:7-8 AMP)*

God wants His children to get better in what they do and get closer to Him. They should pursue excellence in ministry, not for competition or to show superiority or get people's approval, but so that they can please God and be a good example to others.

Paul said, *"Am I now trying to win the favor and approval of men, or of God? Or am I seeking to please someone? If I were still trying to be popular with men, I would not be a bond-servant of Christ."*
Galatians 1:10 AMP

And again Paul said, *"But just as we have been approved by God to be entrusted with the gospel that tells the good news of salvation through faith in Christ, so we speak, not as if we were trying to please people to gain power and popularity, but to please God who examines our hearts expecting our best."*
1 Thessalonians 2:4 AMP

If the motive is wrong, other things will be wrong. Seek to do your best and to be the best, so that God has no reason to look for a replacement for you.

Indeed, we hear that some among you are leading an undisciplined and inappropriate life, doing no work at all, but acting like busybodies [meddling in other people's business]. Now such people we command and exhort in the Lord Jesus Christ to settle down and work quietly and earn their own food and other necessities [supporting themselves instead of depending on the hospitality of others]. And as for [the rest of] you, believers, do not grow

tired or lose heart in doing good [but continue doing what is right without weakening].
2 Thessalonians 3:11-13 AMP

Do your best with what you have to the glory of God whether or not people are watching.

Therefore, whether you eat or drink, or whatever you do, do all to the glory of God.
I Corinthians 10:31 NKJV

Serving God and being our best is never in vain. God is a rewarder of those who diligently seek Him and we will one day stand in His presence to give an account of what we have done on earth.

Therefore, my beloved brothers and sisters, be steadfast, immovable, always excelling in the work of the Lord [always doing your best and doing more than is needed], being continually aware that your labor [even to the point of exhaustion] in the Lord is not futile nor wasted [it is never without purpose].
1 Corinthians 15:58 AMP

Don't be slothful or negligent.

God's Words to Women in Ministry

About Family life

And Adam said: "This is now bone of my bones And flesh of my flesh; She shall be called Woman, Because she was taken out of Man." Therefore a man shall leave his father and mother and be joined to his wife, and they shall become one flesh.
Genesis 2:23-24 NKJV

For I have known him, in order that he may command his children and his household after him, that they keep the way of the Lord, to do righteousness and justice, that the Lord may bring to Abraham what He has spoken to him."
Genesis 18:19 NKJV

And if it seems evil to you to serve the Lord, choose for yourselves this day whom you will serve, whether the gods which your fathers served that were on the other side of the River, or the gods of the Amorites, in whose land you dwell. But as for me and my house, we will serve the Lord."

Joshua 24:15 NKJV

Train up a child in the way he should go, And when he is old he will not depart from it.
Proverbs 22:6 NKJV

She also rises while it is yet night, And provides food for her household, And a portion for her maidservants.
She watches over the ways of her household, And does not eat the bread of idleness.
Her children rise up and call her blessed; Her husband also, and he praises her:
Proverbs 31:15, 27-28 NKJV

And you, fathers, do not provoke your children to wrath, but bring them up in the training and admonition of the Lord.
Ephesians 6:4 NKJV

one who rules his own house well, having his children in submission with all reverence
I Timothy 3:4 NKJV

(for if a man does not know how to rule his own house, how will he take care of the church of God?);
I Timothy 3:5 NKJV

But if anyone does not provide for his own, and especially for those of his household, he has denied the faith and is worse than an unbeliever.
I Timothy 5:8 NKJV

Wives, likewise, be submissive to your own husbands, that even if some do not obey the word, they, without a word, may be won by the conduct of their wives,
I Peter 3:1 NKJV

Words of encouragement

They brought in the ark of the Lord and set it in its place inside the tent which David had pitched for it; and David offered burnt offerings and peace offerings before the Lord.
When David had finished offering the burnt offerings and peace offerings, he blessed the people in the name of the Lord of hosts (armies),
and distributed to all the people, the entire multitude of Israel, both to men and women, to each a [ring-shaped] loaf of bread, a cake of dates, and a cake of raisins. Then all the people departed, each to his house.
Then David returned to bless his household. ...
2 Samuel 6:17-20 AMP

Verse 20 reveals that David returned to bless his household. That's awesome!

Woman in ministry, as you're attending to your ministry, you should attend to your family too. As you bless the people you're ministering to, bless your family too.

If you're married and you have children, don't let your relationship with your husband or children suffer because of your ministry. Create time for them.

In the novel *Tears on My Pillow,* I dealt with the issue of priority. While counselling a married man, a pastor said, "Okay Fred … I want you to write these things I will mention in order of priority to you … let's say about a month ago, when you were having misunderstandings with your wife."

Fred nodded, poised with the pen and paper, waiting for the pastor to continue.
"They are - your kids, God, your mother, your wife, your job, your friends, … what's that girl's name?"
"Who sir?"
"The girl you were seeing, what's her name?"
"Onome."
"Yes. So, write them in their order of importance - your kids, your God, your mother, your wife, your job, your friends, and Onome."
Fred's mouth twisted at the corners in a smile as he bent his head and began to write.
He looked up and asked the pastor, still smiling, "Did you say then or now?"
"Then,"
Fred continued to write and about a minute after, he put the pen down. "I'm through."
"Give it to me." The pastor said, reaching out his hand.
Fred gave the paper to him.
The pastor looked at it and smiled. "Hmm … you have written here: your job, your kids, your friends, your God, your mother, your wife … what about the girl, Onome? Her name is not here."

Fred shook his head. "She shouldn't be on the list sir. She was a mistake."

Still smiling, the pastor said, "Yes, now you know you shouldn't have been involved with her but I'm sure she mattered to you at that time and that was why you started the affair. So, where would she have been on your list?"

Feeling ashamed of himself, Fred smiled, "She wasn't a priority even then. She just happened."

"She wasn't a priority yet you got involved with her!" The pastor said disbelievingly. "That is the problem. People just do things because they feel like. Anyway, based on this list, can you see why you had problems in your marriage and in your life? Your job came first!"

Fred smiled and looked on.

"Your job came first!" The pastor repeated. "Your job came before your wife, your kids, and even your God! So, even though your wife had faults, you were at fault too. Your wife is at the bottom of your list. How could you expect her to be happy?" He stared at Fred.

He cleared his throat and continued, "Even your friends came before her. You definitely neglected her; there was no care, no love. She had been treating you the way you had been treating her. If she had done some things, she had simply been responding to your treatment of her."

Fred nodded in understanding.

The pastor was still talking, "Worse still, your job and friends came before God. It doesn't work that way. If God is not in the first place, the person has made a mistake. The person will be making avoidable mistakes. You know, there are some mistakes that can be avoided but a person who doesn't have God will just plunge in. Nothing will work.

And I am sure you were not happy all that time."

Fred smiled and nodded in agreement with the pastor.

"But I must say that I commend your honesty in helping to resolve these conflicts. Now, there's something you must know, if God is not number one, there can't be happiness. There is a saying - no Christ no peace, know Christ, know peace. He's the Prince of peace. Now, I'm not condemning you, I've also made some of these mistakes like neglecting my wife and stuff."

Fred wondered if the pastor had ever been attracted to another woman since he married.

"But I've never been unfaithful to my wife; I've never been involved with another woman." The pastor said.

Fred was surprised. It was as if the pastor had read his mind.

The pastor continued, "Girlfriends complicate matters. She could get pregnant! And -" he tapped his finger, "that is it! The whole thing turns upside down. People who shouldn't marry each other end up marrying for the sake of peace. Some men would send their wives out for the sake of the new lady. Some men end up with more than one wife. And let me tell you, polygamy can be complicated. It has a higher tendency of aggravating hostility and disunity within the family, both while the man is alive and after his death. Family members suffer; they sometimes go diabolical, spiritually attacking each other."

Fred nodded. "You are right Sir. One of my uncles called me before I married. He said the only regret he had in life was that he had more than one wife."

The pastor nodded, "Even a well-known businessman and politician who is now late said the only mistake he made which he regretted till he died was to have more than one wife. It's a big problem! So, a man has to be careful."

He took a pen, "Now, if your life and marriage will be what it's supposed to be, this is what your priority list should look like."

He took another paper and was talking as he wrote. "The first on the list should be God. Next should be your wife. That is why the Bible says he who loves his wife loves himself. It's a great mystery."

Fred smiled.

The pastor went on, "As the husband, you should nurture and strengthen her. In actual fact, it's for your benefit because if you don't do that, your prayer will be hindered."

Fred nodded.

"You must create time for her. There is no other way to it. If you ask people who have good marriages, they will tell you they create time for each other. As busy as I am, I create time for my wife too. I will sit down and we will talk and review the day together. And when we talk, I don't watch TV, I listen. You have to give her time."

Fred nodded again.

"And you should also handle your sex life."

"My wife is the problem." Fred was quick to say.

"Both of you are the problem. Many women respond to their husbands' treatment of them. So all you need to do is handle her with care and she will respond well."

"Yes Pastor."

"Back to your priority list, next should be your kids and others." The pastor coughed before he said, "So that is it.

Let me talk with your wife for some minutes as well. Go and sit at the reception and call her for me."

Therefore, Woman in ministry, there should be a balance between your family and the ministry. Attend to your ministry and attend to your family. This will help your home, and also help your children to love the Lord and ministry. Be a good wife and mother, and if you're still single, be a good person.

Do what the word of God says you should do about your family. Be a good example to people around you.
In church or wherever I had to minister, I did what I had to do, but at home, I was fully a wife to my husband and a mother to my children.

There was a time I returned home from a church event. As tired as I was, I noticed that one of my children was not in the living room. I asked the others where their 12 year-old sister was and when they said she was in her bedroom, I got up and went there. I opened the door and saw her lying in bed, reading a book. She greeted me. I could have simply responded to her greeting and left the room, but I went to her and asked to see the book. I discovered it was a romantic book, the kind she wasn't supposed to read. She said a friend in school gave it to her. I corrected her and told her that the book must be returned to the friend the next day in school.

Don't just create time for your family, show interest in what they are doing. If I had not gone into my daughter's room, I would not have known what she was doing, and she would have finished reading the book and gotten another one from the friend.

As earlier said in this book, there's nothing you cannot pray about. Pray and ask God to give you wisdom and strength, and ask Him to help you to cope with all that you have to do.

God wants you to have it all – ministry, family, business, and whatever else you're trusting God for, for with God all things are possible.

Don't let satan steal your family from you. Be wise, be strong, and do things right.

Don't allow sex scandal in your life. And if you have made some mistakes along the line, correct the mistakes as necessary, and ensure they are not repeated.

Just as you want to please God in ministry, please God in your home too. And if your home will be okay, your marriage must be okay first. You should submit to your husband.

Wives, submit to your own husbands, as is fitting in the Lord.
Colossians 3:18 NKJV

As I mentioned in the novel *Tears on my pillow*, God must come first, then your family, and then ministry.

Let your husband and children know that they matter to you. Cover them with prayers, and love.

If you're having challenges in your marriage, get help immediately. Go to your spiritual parent for proper counselling. Again, don't let satan steal your family from you.

I'd also like to say that unless your life is in danger, don't seek to separate from your spouse.

I pass this command along (not really I, but the Lord): A wife shouldn't leave her husband. If she does, she should stay single or make up with her husband. Likewise, a husband should not divorce his wife.
1 Corinthians 7:10-11 GW

If you're separated from your husband, make up with your husband as much as possible. If you can't, then stay single as Paul instructed in verse 11 above.

If you don't have a husband, remain a good Christian and live right. Stay away from immoralities and everything that can taint your ministry. The Lord is at hand.

Satan will not outwit you in Jesus' name.

God's Words to Women in Ministry

About Fasting

Then Esther told them to reply to Mordecai: "Go, gather all the Jews who are present in Shushan, and fast for me; neither eat nor drink for three days, night or day. My maids and I will fast likewise. And so I will go to the king, which is against the law; and if I perish, I perish!" Esther 4:15-16 NKJV

Is this not the fast that I have chosen: To loose the bonds of wickedness, To undo the heavy burdens, To let the oppressed go free, And that you break every yoke? Isaiah 58:6 NKJV

Consecrate a fast, call a sacred assembly; Gather the elders And all the inhabitants of the land Into the house of the Lord your God, And cry out to the Lord. Joel 1:14 NKJV

Moreover, when you fast, do not be like the hypocrites, with a sad countenance. For they disfigure their faces that they

*may appear to men to be fasting. Assuredly, I say to you,
they have their reward.
But you, when you fast, anoint your head and wash your
face,
so that you do not appear to men to be fasting, but to your
Father who is in the secret place; and your Father who sees
in secret will reward you openly.
Matthew 6:16-18 NKJV*

*And when He had come into the house, His disciples asked
Him privately, "Why could we not cast it out?"
So, He said to them, "This kind can come out by nothing
but prayer and fasting."
Mark 9:28-29 NKJV*

*and this woman was a widow of about eighty-four years,
who did not depart from the temple, but served God with
fastings and prayers night and day.
Luke 2:37 NKJV*

*being tempted for forty days by the devil. And in those days,
He ate nothing, and afterward, when they had ended, He
was hungry.
Luke 4:2 NKJV*

*Then, having fasted and prayed, and laid hands on them,
they sent them away.
Acts 13:3 NKJV*

*Do not deprive one another except with consent for a time,
that you may give yourselves to fasting and prayer; and*

come together again so that Satan does not tempt you because of your lack of self-control. (I Corinthians 7:5 NKJV)

Words of encouragement

In the novel, *Is It Me You're Looking For*, I wrote:

After service on Sunday, Jite went to the pastor.

He asked her some questions, counselled, and prayed for her. And then he told her to fast and pray for three days, breaking the fast in the evening at six.

Three days? She wondered aloud.

He smiled. "Yes, three days. You've never fasted for three days?"

She smiled and shook her head.

"It's not so easy to fast, I must admit. What I do is what you should do and that is to pray that the Holy Spirit will strengthen you. You need to fast. It will help you in this case."

She nodded.

He gave her three Scriptures, one for each day, to stand on in prayer.

Jite thanked him and left.

On the way home, she was wondering about the fast. She didn't like to fast which was why she rarely joined in the church's fasting. She could still manage to do a day but three days, to break at six in the evening?! How would she do it? And must it be three days?

Well, as she hadn't planned to fast, she wouldn't be able to start tomorrow. She decided to start on Tuesday morning.

On Tuesday morning, she woke up hungry.

"Ah," she moaned. She would have to eat. The fasting would have to start tomorrow.

In the evening, she went to church again for prayer meeting, and this time, it was the pastor's wife who stood when it was time for exhortation.

The woman told the congregation that she would be speaking on the power of fasting.

In the brief exhortation, the woman read three Scriptures and explained them.

Jite was quickly taking notes in her notebook.

The fourth Scripture she read was Matthew 17:21, and then looking at the people, she said, "Jesus told His disciples, 'This kind, this challenge, this crisis, can only be removed by prayer and fasting!'"

The woman went on. "And so, fasting is what you should do when troubles erupt in your life. The trouble may be about your health, marriage, ministry, finance, God's plans for your life, or children. Quite a number of people have heard a lot said about the power of prayer but not much about the power of fasting. And maybe fasting is what you need to do to remove the trouble in your life, to remove that mountain that is standing between you and your miracle."

Jite listened carefully.

The woman continued talking, and then she read Isaiah chapter fifty eight, from verse one to six. Looking up from the Bible, she told them, "Why should you fast? It is to make your voice heard on high."

Jite took a deep breath. She knew fasting was powerful but she didn't know it was this powerful and important. It seemed this was what she had to do. She would fast. She must fast, pray, and seek God's face for her life and future. A lot was at stake. Her future was at stake! She would start tomorrow and as the Assistant Pastor suggested, she would ask God to strengthen her to do it.

On Wednesday morning, Jite didn't eat before leaving for school. During break, she took her Bible and opened it to the book of Psalms chapter forty six, verse nine, one of the Scriptures that the Assistant Pastor gave her.

God makes wars cease to the end of the earth;
He breaks the bow and cuts the spear in two;
He burns the chariot in the fire.

She meditated on it and then began to pray, asking God to intervene in her situation.

Fasting is to stay away from food for a certain period of time because of what the person wants God to do.

It's not easy to fast and quite a number of Christians don't like to fast but this is something that Christians need to do regularly, especially ministers of the gospel as it is beneficial.

Fasting is not directly commanded in the Bible but it is implied that it is a spiritual discipline that Christians will need to observe.

Fasting instils discipline in you. You are learning to master (take control of) your flesh as you deny it of food and focus on your spirit man. As you fast, it strengthens your faith as you are now forced to draw strength from God and not from food. It helps you to focus on God.

In *Matthew 6:16-18*, Jesus told His disciples, "When you fast," not if you fast, to show that they would be expected to fast.

In *Luke 4:2*, Jesus Himself fasted, giving us an example to follow. And when His disciples could not cast out a demon, He made them know that some kind of spirits and situations can be forced out only by prayer and fasting. (*Mark 9:28-29*)

As a Christian who is living for God and serving Him, you are fighting, *not against flesh and blood, but against principalities, against powers, against the rulers of the darkness of this world, and against spiritual wickedness in high places. (Ephesians 6:12)*

The fact that you're a Christian is a problem for satan, and when a Christian begins to fulfill his or her purpose, satan will definitely want to resist the person and the purpose. Satan will not want you to set his captives free.

To overcome and overpower him, you must put on the whole armor of God - all the armor that God supplies, that you may be able to stand against the strategies of the devil. (*Ephesians 6:11*)

Putting on the whole armor enables you to enter the strong man's house, bind him, and plunder his goods. (*Mark 3:27*)

You should also seek God's face with fasting and prayer when you need to make an important decision. Ezra fasted and prayed for divine direction and protection.

Then I proclaimed a fast there at the river of Ahava, that we might humble ourselves before our God, to seek from Him the right way for us and our little ones and all our possessions.
Ezra 8:21 NKJV

When you fast, spend time to pray, read your Bible, meditate, worship, and focus on God. Without these things, you are merely dieting.

You should fast as you feel led by God to do, regularly.
Put on the whole armour of God.

Gods Words to Women in Ministry

About Finances- borrowing and buying on credit

For the Lord your God will bless you just as He promised you; you shall lend to many nations, but you shall not borrow; you shall reign over many nations, but they shall not reign over you.
Deuteronomy 15:6 NKJV

The rich rules over the poor, And the borrower is servant to the lender.
Proverbs 22:7 NKJV

Bring all the tithes into the storehouse, That there may be food in My house, And try Me now in this," Says the Lord of hosts, "If I will not open for you the windows of heaven And pour out for you such blessing That there will not be room enough to receive it.

"And I will rebuke the devourer for your sakes, So that he will not destroy the fruit of your ground, Nor shall the vine fail to bear fruit for you in the field," Says the Lord of hosts; "And all nations will call you blessed, For you will be a delightful land," Says the Lord of hosts.
Malachi 3:10-12 NKJV

Therefore I say to you, do not worry about your life, what you will eat or what you will drink; nor about your body, what you will put on. Is not life more than food and the body more than clothing?
But seek first the kingdom of God and His righteousness, and all these things shall be added to you.
Matthew 6:25, 33 NKJV

Now these are the ones sown among thorns; they are the ones who hear the word,
and the cares of this world, the deceitfulness of riches, and the desires for other things entering in choke the word, and it becomes unfruitful.
Mark 4:18-19 NKJV

And He said to them, "Take heed and beware of covetousness, for one's life does not consist in the abundance of the things he possesses."
Luke 12:15 NKJV

Not that I speak in regard to need, for I have learned in whatever state I am, to be content:

I know how to be abased, and I know how to abound. Everywhere and in all things, I have learned both to be full and to be hungry, both to abound and to suffer need. I can do all things through Christ who strengthens me. Philippians 4:11-13 NKJV

And my God shall supply all your need according to His riches in glory by Christ Jesus. Philippians 4:19 NKJV

Now godliness with contentment is great gain. For we brought nothing into this world, and it is certain we can carry nothing out. And having food and clothing, with these we shall be content. But those who desire to be rich fall into temptation and a snare, and into many foolish and harmful lusts which drown men in destruction and perdition. For the love of money is a root of all kinds of evil, for which some have strayed from the faith in their greediness, and pierced themselves through with many sorrows. But you, O man of God, flee these things and pursue righteousness, godliness, faith, love, patience, gentleness. I Timothy 6:6-11 NKJV

Let your conduct be without covetousness; be content with such things as you have. For He Himself has said, "I will never leave you nor forsake you." Hebrews 13:5 NKJV

Words of encouragement

In the novel *The Forever Kind of Love*, I wrote:

Dayo could see that the five dress shirts were of high quality, but he liked two best. He eventually picked one of the two shirts.

"Why don't you take the second one as well? You can pay for it at the end of the month." Mercy suggested, putting the emerald green shirt in a plastic bag.

"I don't like buying things on credit. I buy what I can afford." He said, collecting the bag from her.

"I don't like doing it myself, but I think there are times it might be necessary." Mercy responded.

"If it's not a matter of life and death or very necessary, I'd rather wait until I can afford it." He said, paying for the shirt.

Mercy learned a good lesson there.

And that is a lesson for you to learn, dear woman in ministry.

As Christians, especially people in ministry, God must be involved in all areas of our lives, including our finances. Just as a Christian has to trust God to meet his or her needs, a woman in ministry must also trust God to provide for her needs. Avoid sinful compromises.

Also, guard against covetousness!

And Jesus said to them, "Take heed and beware of covetousness, for one's life does not consist in the abundance of the things he possesses."
Luke 12:15 NKJV

As much as possible, do not borrow or buy things on credit. If you must borrow money, be careful. Don't borrow it to satisfy current desires. Don't borrow money to buy clothes, shoes, handbags, jewelries, etc, and don't buy these items on credit. Learn how to maximize your earnings and improve on bad spending habits.

God is able to provide for you and increase your possessions!

And my God shall supply all your need according to His riches in glory by Christ Jesus.
Philippians 4:19 NKJV

God's desire is for His people to be a blessing. He wants them to have more than enough and be able to give to others, but you can't give if you're in debt.

Give to him who asks you, and from him who wants to borrow from you do not turn away.
Matthew 5:42 NKJV

If you must borrow, let it be for a reasonable need. Don't borrow to spend on frivolities.

In addition, if you must borrow, be sure you will be able to repay the amount borrowed, and on time! The Bible calls a person who borrows and does not pay back wicked.

The wicked borrows and does not repay, But the righteous shows mercy and gives.
Psalms 37:21 NKJV

If for any reason you won't be able to repay on time or it has to be paid in instalments, let the lender be aware. Discuss with the lender about a payment plan ahead of time. Agree on the terms of repayment, and make your payments on time, without delay.

Furthermore, if after careful consideration, taking a loan is the only way out, involve God as with everything else by praying first and asking for directions. Then decide how much you need to borrow, the repayment plan, and then trust God to help you pay back your loan on time.

Another important factor in handling your finances is learning how to budget effectively in order to live within your means. Having a budget would reveal bad spending habits and also ensure you don't spend money that you don't have. With the help of the Holy Spirit and careful planning, creating a budget that works can be achieved and you will not be in debt.

The Bible encourages whoever lacks wisdom to ask God.

But let patience have its perfect work, that you may be perfect and complete, lacking nothing.
If any of you lacks wisdom, let him ask of God, who gives to all liberally and without reproach, and it will be given to him.
But let him ask in faith, with no doubting, for he who doubts is like a wave of the sea driven and tossed by the wind.
For let not that man suppose that he will receive anything from the Lord;
he is a double-minded man, unstable in all his ways.
James 1:4-8 NKJV

Additionally, whenever you can, save, save, save. From your earnings, after paying your tithe and other essentials such as rent, food; if it's not in your budget and it's a non-essential item, forgo it and save the rest of what you have. The saying goes "a little drop makes a might ocean". A few cash here and there, would eventually add up to a fortune.

Paying tithe is important for financial blessing. God has instructed us in the Bible to give a tenth of our earnings to Him; men and women in ministry are not exempted from this rule. The Bible says a lot about these things and I pointed them out in some of my novels, such as *Then Came You*.

After the call, Bode took the envelope that Joseph gave him, opened it and was surprised when he saw how much cash was in it. He had not expected much from a students' fellowship.

Removing his tithe, he pocketed the remaining money, and as he alighted from the car, he smiled. The money might come handy at the store, he told himself but almost immediately, he could hear the voice of God caution him: Why must you spend the money? Why can't you save it?

Alright, yes Lord.

In conclusion, whether you have to take out a loan or you are able to budget and save, the ultimate rule is to hear from God and be led concerning your finances. Obeying His instructions and being wise is the way into abundance.

Don't let satan have a hold over you by controlling your finances. Take charge!

God's Words to Women in Ministry

About Focus

They looked to Him and were radiant; Their faces will never blush in shame or confusion.
Psalms 34:5 AMP

I have inclined my heart to perform Your statutes Forever, to the very end.
Psalms 119:112 NKJV

Let your eyes look straight ahead, And your eyelids look right before you.
Ponder the path of your feet, And let all your ways be established.
Do not turn to the right or the left; Remove your foot from evil.
Proverbs 4:25-27 NKJV

"For the Lord God will help Me; Therefore I will not be disgraced; Therefore I have set My face like a flint, And I know that I will not be ashamed.
Isaiah 50:7 NKJV

Then the twelve summoned the multitude of the disciples and said, "It is not desirable that we should leave the word of God and serve tables.
Therefore, brethren, seek out from among you seven men of good reputation, full of the Holy Spirit and wisdom, whom we may appoint over this business;
but we will give ourselves continually to prayer and to the ministry of the word."
Acts 6:2-4 NKJV

Brethren, I do not count myself to have apprehended; but one thing I do, forgetting those things which are behind and reaching forward to those things which are ahead, I press toward the goal for the prize of the upward call of God in Christ Jesus.
Philippians 3:13-14 NKJV

Set your mind on things above, not on things on the earth.
Colossians 3:2 NKJV

Till I come, give attention to reading, to exhortation, to doctrine.
Meditate on these things; give yourself entirely to them, that your progress may be evident to all.

Take heed to yourself and to the doctrine. Continue in them, for in doing this you will save both yourself and those who hear you.
I Timothy 4:13, 15-16 NKJV

looking unto Jesus, the author and finisher of our faith, who for the joy that was set before Him endured the cross, despising the shame, and has sat down at the right hand of the throne of God.
Hebrews 12:2 NKJV

Words of encouragement

You need to focus on your ministry which is your divine purpose.

As I mentioned in the book *God's Words to Older Adults*:

1)A divine purpose can be frustrated.

"Then the people of the land discouraged the people of Judah and made them afraid to build and bribed counsellors against them to frustrate their purpose, all the days of Cyrus king of Persia, even until the reign of Darius king of Persia."
Ezra 4:4-5

2)A person can be withdrawn from his or her purpose.

"That He may turn man aside from his deed and conceal pride from a man;"
Job 33:17

3)Purposes can be disappointed or established.

"Without counsel plans fail, but with many advisers they succeed."
Proverbs 15:22 ESV

4)And a purpose can be established and fulfilled.

Jesus, Paul, Moses, Samuel, were some of the people in the Bible who fulfilled their purposes, while Samson, Saul, Judas Iscariot, were among those who allowed their destinies to be truncated.

The people who fulfilled their purposes had some things in common, and one of them is – focus. They were focused on God and their purpose.

And one of the things that the people whose destinies were truncated had in common was distraction.

I sometimes hear some people in ministry admit that they have been distracted. However, what people call a distraction is actually satan at work, and those people are yielding to satan's influence. Distractions are satan's way of pulling people away from their divine purpose.

You must be focused on what you believe God has called you do.

Let your eyes look straight ahead, and your eyelids look right before you. Ponder the path of your feet, and let all your ways be established. Do not turn to the right or the left; remove your foot from evil.
(Proverbs 4:25-27 NKJV)

Many voices will call out to you. As God wants you to obey Him, He will speak to you in a bid to get your attention. Satan, as well as people, will also try to get your attention. You must learn to discern whose voice is speaking at each point in time, and choose to obey only the voice of God.

In the Bible, Samson became distracted. He kept yielding to satan and eventually lost everything.

Satan's plan is to steal, kill, and destroy your ministry, don't let him succeed. He tries to make people forget what is really important and make them begin to chase shadows. Don't be deceived.

Don't forget that you're in ministry to get people saved and live for God. Whatever you're doing, whether singing or preaching or acting, or whatever the ministry is about, it should not be to entertain people but to proclaim the gospel of Jesus. Do all to the glory of God.

Therefore, whether you eat or drink, or whatever you do, do all to the glory of God.
I Corinthians 10:31 NKJV

Regularly ask yourself, *why am I here? Why am I doing what I am doing? Is this what God wants me to do? Am I doing it right?*

Focus on your ministry, and focus on God - let Him be your strength.

Paul said, *"Brethren, I do not count myself to have apprehended; but one thing I do, forgetting those things which are behind and reaching forward to those things which are ahead, I press toward the goal for the prize of the upward call of God in Christ Jesus." (Philippians 3:13-14 NKJV)*

The Bible says a lot about time. Be careful how you spend your time, don't let it be wasted. Keep in mind that a time is coming when you will not be able to work again. *(John 9:4)*

Do all you can now so that at the end of time, you won't have cause for regrets and would be able to say like Timothy did - *I have fought the good fight, I have finished the race, I have kept the faith. (II Timothy 4:7-8)*

Jesus too kept the faith to the end, refusing to be distracted. When someone from the crowd said to Him, *"Teacher, tell my brother to divide the inheritance with me." Jesus answered him, "Man, who made Me a judge or an arbitrator over you?" (Luke 12:13-14 NKJV)*

He knew that His purpose was to preach the good news to people and save them, and He used the opportunity to warn His listeners about covetousness.

Toward the end of His life, He said to His Father, *"I have glorified You on the earth. I have finished the work which You have given Me to do." (John 17:4 NKJV)*

This clearly reveals that it is possible to remain focused and fulfill divine purpose.

Keep your purpose in your heart, always consider what is a priority for you to do, and then do it.

Know what God has called you to do and stay in it. Have a clear focus. If you don't know your ministry or you're not careful, you will be pulled in different directions.

People sometimes contact me to mentor them on writing but no, that is not a part of what God has called me to do, currently, and I tell them so. That is currently not my focus. My calling is to live for God and teach people to live for God in their marriage, relationship, ministry, and life, through writing, counselling, and teaching of the Word. I can't do everything, and I don't try to do everything. There has to be a balance.

Don't try to do everything. Focus on the assignment(s) God has given you.

God's Words to Women in Ministry

About Friendship

Then Elijah said to Elisha, "Stay here, please, for the Lord has sent me on to Bethel." But Elisha said, "As the Lord lives, and as your soul lives, I will not leave you!" So, they went down to Bethel.
II Kings 2:2 NKJV

Now when Job's three friends heard of all this adversity that had come upon him, each one came from his own place—Eliphaz the Temanite, Bildad the Shuhite, and Zophar the Naamathite. For they had made an appointment together to come and mourn with him, and to comfort him.
Job 2:11 NKJV

He who walks with wise men will be wise, But the companion of fools will be destroyed.
Proverbs 13:20 NKJV

He who covers a transgression seeks love, But he who repeats a matter separates friends.

Proverbs 17:9 NKJV

A friend loves at all times, And a brother is born for adversity.
Proverbs 17:17 NKJV

A man who has friends must himself be friendly, But there is a friend who sticks closer than a brother.
Proverbs 18:24 NKJV

Make no friendship with an angry man, And with a furious man do not go, Lest you learn his ways And set a snare for your soul.
Proverbs 22:24-25 NKJV

Faithful are the wounds of a friend, But the kisses of an enemy are deceitful.
Proverbs 27:6 NKJV

Two are better than one, Because they have a good reward for their labor. For if they fall, one will lift up his companion. But woe to him who is alone when he falls, For he has no one to help him up.
Ecclesiastes 4:9-10 NKJV

But now I have written to you not to keep company with anyone named a brother, who is sexually immoral, or covetous, or an idolater, or a reviler, or a drunkard, or an extortioner— not even to eat with such a person.
I Corinthians 5:11 NKJV

Do not be deceived: "Evil company corrupts good habits."
I Corinthians 15:33 NKJV

Words of encouragement

In the novel *The Forever Kind of Love*, I wrote:

Mercy was in her room folding her clothes. When her phone began to ring and she saw that it was Dayo, she stopped what she was doing immediately and answered it. "Hello, Dayo."

"Mercy. I saw your message. What's up?"

"Not much." She sat on her bed near the pillow. "I'm sure you realized that I added a little to the price I gave your friend. The difference is your commission on the sale."

"No, that is not necessary."

"I give commission to people who connect me."

"No, you don't need to give me commission."

"You didn't ask for it, and I know it's not much but don't reject it."

She heard his chuckle.

She spoke again. "They haven't even bought them. Let's hope they do."

"They will." He assured her. "Well, thanks but I can't take commission on this particular one. Joshua is my very good friend. Actually, I have three very close friends: Joshua, Jim, and Wole. The four of us move together and ... do things together. We are like brothers from different mothers. I can't make profit from any of these three guys.

We are close to the extent that assuming Joshua is not able to pay you the money, one of us or all of us will have to cough it out."

"Oh, that's wonderful. Are the others also married?"

"No. Only Joshua is married. The other two are engaged though." He said.

"Well, that's fine. I just wanted you to know about the commission thing." She told him.

"Thanks. I will make sure the other two also patronize you. I can't take commission on the sales to the three of them but if I'm able to link you with some other people, I'll take whatever you give me."

"I understand. I like that kind of friendship. That's wonderful." She told him. She had that kind of friendship with Lekan and Stella as well.

He chuckled and responded to her comment. "We've been friends for some time. Their women are also bonding. I'm meeting with them tomorrow."

"For what?"

"We just try to get together regularly. We spend some time together, talk, share the Scripture and afterward, pray." He said.

In this novel, those three men were Dayo's close friends, and Mercy had Lekan and Stella as close friends.

God does not want us to go through life and ministry alone. At the beginning when He created Adam, He said that it wasn't good for Adam to be alone. Adam needed to have a companion, someone to talk with and confide in.

However, Adam needed an appropriate person, not just anything or just anyone. The Bible says that there was not found a helper comparable to him. God had to create Eve and when Adam saw her, he said, ***"This is now bone of my bones And flesh of my flesh; She shall be called Woman, Because she was taken out of Man."***
Genesis 2:20-23 NKJV

God has surrounded us with people. Everywhere we turn to, there are people who in God's design are there to relate with us and bring us to the level He wants us to be. God has done it in such a way that we need others to even survive in life.

Don't close people out of your life. You should not be a lone ranger, friendship is a blessing. However, you don't need a lot of friends. It's about quality, not quantity.

Friends can influence us to do good or bad, use good words or bad words and curses, get closer to God or draw away from Him, be committed to marriage or seek divorce, succeed in life or be destroyed, and that is why we need to be careful and prayerful. I recently learnt of a lady who used to love the Lord and was very zealous for Him, but through association, she now believes a lot of wrong doctrines, and tells people that it is wrong to pay tithe and there is no reason to go to church to worship God.

Friends can affect our values, behaviors, attitudes and beliefs. Their ways rub off on us and we may begin to emulate them without realizing it as the changes happen subtly and gradually. They also define us, and people think we are like our friends. If you are not like your friends who compromise God's standard, then there's no point hanging around them.

You must have heard these popular sayings: Show me your friends and I will tell you who you are; show me your friends and I will show you your character. These statements are true.

True friends will stand by you, encourage you, and warn you when necessary. They will pray for you, help you, and keep you in check. They can also help you discover who you really are and will tell you the truth, sometimes the truth that you may not want to accept.

Note that I said 'true friends' because there are bad friends, even in ministry and among 'so called ministers'.

Yes, you need friends but you need to be careful because a wrong friend would do you and your ministry more harm than good.

There are some people you should not relate with because they will diminish you. They are not good for you and they should be dumped or kept at an arm's length. By their fruits you shall know them.

As such, let God Who knows the heart of everyone choose your friends for you.

The heart is deceitful above all things, And desperately wicked; Who can know it? I, the Lord , search the heart, I test the mind, Even to give every man according to his ways, According to the fruit of his doings.
Jeremiah 17:9-10 NKJV

Most of the people who left ministry did so because of challenges with people. Bad friends will hurt you. Let the Holy Spirit reveal a true friend to you.

If you're married, your spouse should be one of your friends. And if you're not yet married, keep this in mind - it is often said that the best person to marry is a friend because such a person already knows who you are and has accepted you. However, marrying a friend does not guarantee a good marriage. You will have a good marriage as both the man and his wife yield to God's instructions.

Another thing to keep in mind is this - to have friends, you must be friendly yourself. Be nice without compromising God's standard.

Pray about everything and God will guide you.

God's Words to Women in Ministry

About Gossip

You shall not circulate a false report. Do not put your hand with the wicked to be an unrighteous witness.
Exodus 23:1 NKJV

You shall not go about as a talebearer among your people; nor shall you take a stand against the life of your neighbor: I am the Lord.
Leviticus 19:16 NKJV

Keep your tongue from evil, And your lips from speaking deceit.
Psalms 34:13 NKJV

The words of a talebearer are like tasty trifles, And they go down into the inmost body.
Proverbs 18:8 NKJV

being filled with all unrighteousness, sexual immorality, wickedness, covetousness, maliciousness; full of envy, murder, strife, deceit, evil-mindedness; they are whisperers,
backbiters, haters of God, violent, proud, boasters, inventors of evil things,
disobedient to parents, undiscerning, untrustworthy, unloving, unforgiving, unmerciful;
who, knowing the righteous judgment of God, that those who practice such things are deserving of death, not only do the same but also approve of those who practice them.
Romans 1:29-32 NKJV

For I fear lest, when I come, I shall not find you such as I wish, and that I shall be found by you such as you do not wish; lest there be contentions, jealousies, outbursts of wrath, selfish ambitions, backbitings, whisperings, conceits, tumults;
II Corinthians 12:20 NKJV

Abstain from every form of evil.
I Thessalonians 5:22 NKJV

And besides they learn to be idle, wandering about from house to house, and not only idle but also gossips and busybodies, saying things which they ought not.
I Timothy 5:13 NKJV

Be diligent to present yourself approved to God, a worker who does not need to be ashamed, rightly dividing the word of truth. But shun profane and idle babblings, for they will increase to more ungodliness.
II Timothy 2:15-16 NKJV

If anyone among you thinks he is religious, and does not bridle his tongue but deceives his own heart, this one's religion is useless.
James 1:26 NKJV

With it we bless our God and Father, and with it we curse men, who have been made in the similitude of God. Out of the same mouth proceed blessing and cursing. My brethren, these things ought not to be so.
James 3:9-10 NKJV

Words of encouragement

Don't be a gossip and don't trust a gossip!

A gossip betrays a confidence; so avoid anyone who talks too much.
Proverbs 20:19 NIV

A gossip is a whisperer, a talebearer. This person talks behind people's back in a way that can hurt the people.
How can you tell if you're gossiping? It's a gossip if you have no good reason to reveal or discuss the particular issue with the people you're talking with, and if the subject of the gossip won't be happy to know that he/she's being discussed.

Gossiping can be hurtful to the subject of the gossip. If you wouldn't like people to gossip about you, don't gossip about others. Just as you want men to do to you, you also do to them likewise. *(Luke 6:31 NKJV)*

If you know that the subject of the gossip won't be happy to hear that you've talked about him or her, then don't talk about the person. Let that be a caution to you.

It's possible to gossip without realising it on time, but when you know, stop it. Don't say things you will not be able to defend or repeat in the presence of the subject of the gossip.

Don't gossip about other women in ministry and what they are doing. If you must talk, say things that will encourage everyone around to be better. Let your words bring honour to God, don't be malicious.

When you're with friends, choose to talk about good ideas or positive things that will help your lives and ministries rather than talk about people and how they are living unless the subject of discussion concerns you or you need to bring it up for some good reasons.

If your friends are the ones talking about people, you may choose not to respond but if you must respond, choose your words with care so that you don't get quoted later on. Don't say things that you should not, and be careful who you talk with.

If you have a friend who likes to gossip or badmouth others, try to discourage the person so that you're not influenced to do likewise. You can let the person know in clear terms that you're not interested in the story.

There are other ways of discouraging a gossip.
You can:
change the topic of discussion;
excuse yourself and leave;
don't nod or smile at what is being said;
or let it show in your countenance that you're not interested.
Another way is to avoid the person if the person is a bad influence on you.

Gossiping will make people stop trusting you because they will reason that if you can talk about others, you will definitely talk about them. They won't want to share their concerns with you which is not a good thing for you. This can render your ministry useless.

Satan is the spirit behind gossip, and a gossip is being influenced, saying what satan wants him/her to say without realising it.

Gossiping about others says a lot about you and your spiritual life. Gossiping makes you talk like a person who doesn't know God. The Bible also reveals that it's born out of idleness. (*1Timothy 5:13*)

If you have been guilty of this error, pray, and keep your tongue from speaking evil.

Do not let any unwholesome talk come out of your mouths, but only what is helpful for building others up according to their needs, that it may benefit those who listen.
Ephesians 4:29 NIV

Keep in mind that everyone will have to give account on the day of judgment for every empty word they have spoken. (*Matthew 12:36*)

Therefore, focus on your calling and stay away from sins.

God's Words to Women in Ministry

About the Holy Spirit

When all the people were baptized, it came to pass that Jesus also was baptized; and while He prayed, the heaven was opened. And the Holy Spirit descended in bodily form like a dove upon Him, and a voice came from heaven which said, "You are My beloved Son; in You I am well pleased."
Luke 3:21-22 NKJV

And I will ask the Father, and He will give you another Helper (Comforter, Advocate, Intercessor—Counselor, Strengthener, Standby), to be with you forever—
the Spirit of Truth, whom the world cannot receive [and take to its heart] because it does not see Him or know Him, but you know Him because He (the Holy Spirit) remains with you continually and will be in you.
John 14:16-17 AMP

But the Helper (Comforter, Advocate, Intercessor— Counselor, Strengthener, Standby), the Holy Spirit, whom the Father will send in My name [in My place, to

represent Me and act on My behalf], He will teach you all things. And He will help you remember everything that I have told you.
John 14:26 AMP

"But when the   Helper (Comforter, Advocate, Intercessor—Counselor, Strengthener, Standby) comes, whom I will send to you from the Father, that is the Spirit of Truth who comes from the Father, He will testify and bear witness about Me.
John 15:26 AMP

But I tell you the truth, it is to your advantage that I go away; for if I do not go away, the Helper (Comforter, Advocate, Intercessor—Counselor, Strengthener, Standby) will not come to you; but if I go, I will send Him (the Holy Spirit) to you [to be in close fellowship with you].
John 16:7 AMP

However, when He, the Spirit of truth, has come, He will guide you into all truth; for He will not speak on His own authority, but whatever He hears He will speak; and He will tell you things to come. He will glorify Me, for He will take of what is Mine and declare it to you. All things that the Father has are Mine. Therefore I said that He will take of Mine and declare it to you.
John 16:13-15 NKJV

And when they had prayed, the place where they were assembled together was shaken; and they were all filled

with the Holy Spirit, and they spoke the word of God with boldness.
Acts 4:31 NKJV

For what man knows the things of a man except the spirit of the man which is in him? Even so no one knows the things of God except the Spirit of God.
I Corinthians 2:11 NKJV

And do not grieve the Holy Spirit of God, by whom you were sealed for the day of redemption.
Ephesians 4:30 NKJV

But you, beloved, building yourselves up on your most holy faith, praying in the Holy Spirit,
Jude 1:20 NKJV

Words of encouragement

In the novel *Sea of Regrets*, I wrote:

The General Overseer preached for about an hour, gave an altar call and some people came out. After that, he asked all the ministers to come out so he could pray for them, and Pastor Femi and Pastor Ibie were the first to stand.

While praying for them one after the other, he suddenly stopped, looked at the congregation and said, "I can hear God saying that He's giving some people children."

"Halleluya!" "Amen!" The congregation shouted.

"Those of you who are married and are believing God for children, receive yours in Jesus name!"

"Amen!"

He glanced over the congregation as if looking for someone, then pointing in the direction of Lola and Bori, he said, "That my sister, come."

Lola looked at the people around her, not sure of who he was calling.

"That sister in the flowery red dress and black hat." He said.

Shocked, Lola stood.

"Come."

With shaking legs, she went to the front.

"God is giving you children."

Lola burst into tears.
"Are you married?" He asked.
"Yes."
"How many children do you have?"
Sobbing, she shook her head.
"Glory to God!" He said. "God said He has heard your prayers and is wiping away your tears."
Lola fell down under the anointing.
"Hallelujah! Bring her up! Bring her up!" He said.
The female ministers who were around lifted her ...

What happened in this story was a manifestation of the Holy Spirit. The importance and roles of the Holy Spirit in the life and ministry of 'the called' cannot be overemphasized.

The Holy Spirit is the power of God at work in the life of a believer. He is the third Person in the God Head.

And afterward, I will pour out my Spirit on all people. Your sons and daughters will prophesy, your old men will dream dreams, your young men will see visions. Even on my servants, both men and women, I will pour out my Spirit in those days.
Joel 2:28-29 NIV

The involvement of the Holy Spirit in ministry is so important that He descended on Jesus before Jesus entered the ministry (**Luke 3:22**), and Jesus commanded His disciples to wait until they received the Holy Spirit before going into ministries.

On one occasion, while He was eating with them, He gave them this command: ***Do not leave Jerusalem, but wait for the gift My Father promised, which you have heard Me speak about.***

For John baptized with water, but in a few days you will be baptized with the Holy Spirit.
But you will receive power when the Holy Spirit comes on you; and you will be My witnesses in Jerusalem, and in all Judea and Samaria, and to the ends of the earth.
Acts 1:4-5, 8 NIV

John reveals more about Who the Holy Spirit is to a believer.

Jesus said, "***And I will ask the Father, and He will give you another Helper (Comforter, Advocate, Intercessor—Counselor, Strengthener, Standby), to be with you forever— (John 14:16-17 AMP)***

Knowing that the Holy Spirit is all these and will be with God's people forever is awesome!

The Holy Spirit is also the Spirit of Truth, to live in us and abide with us continually.

the Spirit of Truth, whom the world cannot receive [and take to its heart] because it does not see Him or know Him, but you know Him because He (the Holy Spirit) remains with you continually and will be in you.

John 14:17 AMP

As a woman in ministry, you need to know that the Holy Spirit is a Person, not a thing. As a Person, He can be grieved.

And do not grieve the Holy Spirit of God, with whom you were sealed for the day of redemption.
Ephesians 4:30 NIV

Learn to be aware of the presence of the Holy Spirit and His works.

You also need to learn to walk with Him and be led by Him. God expects you to be led by the Holy Spirit and not by people, circumstances, emotions, sight, or signs, etc, *for those who are led by the Holy Spirit are the true children of God. (Romans 8:14)*

In order to hear and be led by Him, you should be sensitive in the spirit.

The following are some ways to become sensitive to the leading of the Holy Spirit.

1)Learn to fast from time to time,
2)Spend quality time in prayer and meditating on the word of God,
3)Speak in tongues a lot. Jude 1:20 charges us to build ourselves up by praying in the Holy Ghost.
4)Spend time fellowshipping with God,

5)Work on yourself so that your heart becomes tender. It's a tender heart that can pick up the nudging of the Holy Spirit and what the Holy Spirit is saying.

Allow the Holy Spirit to lead you in all things.

God's Words to Women in Ministry

About Loving even the difficult people

Hatred stirs up strife, But love covers all sins.
Proverbs 10:12 NKJV

A soft answer turns away wrath, But a harsh word stirs
up anger.
Proverbs 15:1 NKJV

But I say to you who hear: Love your enemies, do good to
those who hate you,
bless those who curse you, and pray for those who
spitefully use you.
To him who strikes you on the one cheek, offer the other
also. And from him who takes away your cloak, do not
withhold your tunic either.
"But if you love those who love you, what credit is that to
you? For even sinners love those who love them.
And if you do good to those who do good to you, what
credit is that to you? For even sinners do the same.
But love your enemies, do good, and lend, hoping for
nothing in return; and your reward will be great, and you

will be sons of the Most High. For He is kind to the unthankful and evil.
Therefore be merciful, just as your Father also is merciful.
Luke 6:27-29, 32-33, 35-36 NKJV

By this all will know that you are My disciples, if you have love for one another."
John 13:35 NKJV

This is My commandment, that you love one another as I have loved you.
John 15:12 NKJV

For all the law is fulfilled in one word, even in this: "You shall love your neighbor as yourself." But if you bite and devour one another, beware lest you be consumed by one another!
Galatians 5:14-15 NKJV

But avoid foolish and ignorant disputes, knowing that they generate strife.
And a servant of the Lord must not quarrel but be gentle to all, able to teach, patient, in humility correcting those who are in opposition,
if God perhaps will grant them repentance, so that they may know the truth,
and that they may come to their senses and escape the snare of the devil, having been taken captive by him to do his will.
II Timothy 2:23-26 NKJV

not returning evil for evil or reviling for reviling, but on the contrary blessing, knowing that you were called to this, that you may inherit a blessing.
I Peter 3:9 NKJV

Words of encouragement

Some people are easy to love. They are pleasant and easy going. You just love them, especially if you have relationship in mind. You love them because they love you.

But sometimes you meet people who are not so nice, who are difficult to love. They get on your nerves; you don't like them much and you want to avoid them.

These people are not always strangers however, and they are everywhere. They are in your school, at your workplace, in your church. They are even in your family! The difficult person may be your spouse, child, sibling, parent-in-law.

The word of God is clear though. *"But I say to you who hear: Love your enemies, do good to those who hate you, bless those who curse you, and pray for those who spitefully use you."*
Luke 6:27-28 NKJV

"If you only love those who love you, what credit is that to you? For even sinners love those who love them."
Luke 6:32 AMP

In the Bible, the children of Israel were an example of difficult people. Instead of being grateful to God and Moses for bringing them out of bondage in Egypt, they were disobedient and complained about almost everything - water, food, etc.

But Moses remained patient, interceding on their behalf so they would not be destroyed.

This is how to love difficult people. Be patient with them, love them, and pray for them.

He who does not love does not know God, for God is love. I John 4:8 NKJV

Some of the things that difficult people do are mentioned in **Luke 6:27-29**: difficult people may hate you, curse, mistreat, slap you. They may resist you, disrespect you, be argumentative.

In Love on the Pulpit, Mrs. Coker was a difficult wife.

Mr. Coker laughed and cleared his throat. "If anything seems to last or is working, God is somewhere there, because satan doesn't have any good plan for anybody. So, it has been by the grace of God. Now, as you said, my wife is - a woman like a man, so how have I coped? When I was going into the marriage, I made up my mind it was going to be for a lifetime, no matter what, I would not divorce my wife. And God has helped me with that, although, many times, I've been tempted to change my mind."

117

The people laughed.

He continued. "What young people need to know is that there's no marriage that doesn't have ups and downs, so my advice is - just stay together and work through your problems. Remarrying is not the solution, because the new person is not perfect too. When I feel offended, I call her and express my feelings. But in all, we have to thank God ... and our children have been wonderful too."

How to handle them
*Love them,
*do good to them,
*bless them,
*pray for them,
*give to them.
*You can also correct or rebuke them when necessary, let them know what the Bible says, and be silent.

As pointed out in *1Peter 3:9 NKJV, don't return evil for evil or reviling for reviling, but on the contrary blessing, knowing that you were called to this, that you may inherit a blessing.*

As a woman in ministry, you might even notice that some people are unpleasant to you but pleasant to your husband or other church members. It is quite common to see this happen; however, you should not let this change your attitude. You still have to be kind. Show love. Do not put on a show, let it come from your heart. This is where you pray and ask God to help you to love them.

Furthermore, take time to evaluate yourself. Are you pleasant to be around? This is the reminder you need to pray that you will walk in the spirit so that you don't become a difficult person. Watch what you say, your body language, your facial expressions, your actions.

Be patient with difficult people.

God's Words to Women in Ministry

About Personal Development

Your word is a lamp to my feet and a light to my path.
Psalms 119:105 NKJV

As for these four young men, God gave them knowledge
and skill in all literature and wisdom; and Daniel had
understanding in all visions and dreams.
Daniel 1:17 NKJV

And the Child grew and became strong in spirit, filled
with wisdom; and the grace of God was upon Him. And
Jesus increased in wisdom and stature, and in favour with
God and men.
Luke 2:40, 52 NKJV

So, Philip ran to him, and heard him reading the prophet
Isaiah, and said, "Do you understand what you are
reading?"
And he said, "How can I, unless someone guides me?"
And he asked Philip to come up and sit with him.
Acts 8:30-31 NKJV

Be diligent to present yourself approved to God, a worker who does not need to be ashamed, rightly dividing the word of truth. But shun profane and idle babblings, for they will increase to more ungodliness.
II Timothy 2:15 NKJV

All Scripture is given by inspiration of God, and is profitable for doctrine, for reproof, for correction, for instruction in righteousness,
that the man of God may be complete, thoroughly equipped for every good work.
II Timothy 3:16-17 NKJV

For though by this time you ought to be teachers, you need someone to teach you again the first principles of the oracles of God; and you have come to need milk and not solid food.
For everyone who partakes only of milk is unskilled in the word of righteousness, for he is a babe.
But solid food belongs to those who are of full age, that is, those who by reason of use have their senses exercised to discern both good and evil.
Hebrews 5:12-14 NKJV

but grow in the grace and knowledge of our Lord and Saviour Jesus Christ. To Him be the glory both now and forever. Amen.
II Peter 3:18 NKJV

Words of encouragement

As a person and especially as a woman in ministry, you need to keep growing and getting better. This is because you're working for God, and ministry is about leading people and drawing them closer to God, but how can you give what you don't have?

At about the age of 17, one of my lecturers said in class – *you cannot give what you don't have.* This phrase made so much sense to me and stuck in my brain.
When I became a Christian later at age 20 and began to study the Scriptures, I found out that some Scriptures support that phrase.
The following are some of them.

For if there is first a willing mind, it is accepted according to what one has, and not according to what he does not have.
II Corinthians 8:12 NKJV

And you shall love the Lord your God with all your heart, with all your soul, with all your mind, and with all your strength.
This is the first commandment. And the second, like it, is this: 'You shall love your neighbour as yourself.' There is no other commandment greater than these.

Mark 12:30-31 NKJV

How can you love another person if you don't love yourself? How can you lead people to Christ if you don't have Christ or if you are spiritually dry?

Therefore, to be effective in ministry, you need to keep learning and growing in the things of God and the things that will make you effective.

Jesus fasted for 40 days which was a part of His personal development, and shortly after, the anointing on Him was obvious for everyone to see.

At a time, He went down to Capernaum, a city of Galilee, and was teaching the people on the Sabbaths. And they were astonished at His teaching, for His word was with authority.

At another time, He went into the synagogue where a demon possessed man encountered Him.

Now in the synagogue there was a man who had a spirit of an unclean demon. And he cried out with a loud voice, saying, "Let us alone! What have we to do with You, Jesus of Nazareth? Did You come to destroy us? I know who You are— the Holy One of God!"
But Jesus rebuked him, saying, "Be quiet, and come out of him!" And when the demon had thrown him in their midst, it came out of him and did not hurt him.

Then they were all amazed and spoke among themselves, saying, "What a word this is! For with authority and power He commands the unclean spirits, and they come out."
Luke 4:31-36 NKJV

Some of the things you need to do are:

*Spend quality time studying the word of God and in prayer.
*Walk with the wise and you shall be wise.
*Ask questions from the right people.
*Read good books.
*Attend edifying seminars, listen to godly preachers and people who are good.
*Learn how to do what you're doing well.

In a bid to learn, don't become obsessed to the extent that you become distracted, however. You're not in competition with anyone or with the world. Your development is so that you can be more like Jesus and serve God better. Our God is an excellent God.

Another thing to do is to have a retreat as necessary. Jesus also observed this as He often withdrew to a solitary place to pray.

And in the novel *The Forever Kind of Love*, Pastor Femi and his wife, Pastor Ibie went for their church's retreat. In the book, I wrote: Ibie and Femi slept and woke up at eight-thirty. They got ready and left for the hall for the first session.

The meeting began at nine prompt with prayers, led by one of the pastors. This was followed by praise and worship session. Then the G.O.'s wife gave the welcome address before the G.O. collected the microphone. He talked about the importance of the retreat before encouraging and sharing the Scripture with the over fifty ministers who were present.

The following are some of the benefits of proper growth:

*Proper growth prevents stagnation.
*It makes you avoid mediocrity.
*It will also make you grow in God's grace,
*It will increase your value,
*Make you remain relevant.
*It will help you to be good in what you do.

If a person is not growing and getting better, he or she will be limited, and the effectiveness will also be limited.

Have a plan on how you want to achieve the growth and follow through.

God's Words to Women in Ministry

About Prayer

Then you will call upon Me and go and pray to Me, and I will listen to you.
Jeremiah 29:12

But you, when you pray, go into your room, and when you have shut your door, pray to your Father who is in the secret place; and your Father who sees in secret will reward you openly.
Matthew 6:6

Therefore I say to you, whatever things you ask when you pray, believe that you receive them, and you will have them.
Mark 11:24

When all the people were baptized, it came to pass that Jesus also was baptized; and while He prayed, the heaven was opened.
Luke 3:21

*So I say to you, ask, and it will be given to you; seek, and
you will find; knock, and it will be opened to you.
For everyone who asks receives, and he who seeks finds,
and to him who knocks it will be opened.
If a son asks for bread from any father among you, will
he give him a stone? Or if he asks for a fish, will he give
him a serpent instead of a fish?
Or if he asks for an egg, will he offer him a scorpion?
If you then, being evil, know how to give good gifts to
your children, how much more will your heavenly Father
give the Holy Spirit to those who ask Him!
Luke 11:9-13*

*Then He spoke a parable to them, that men always ought
to pray and not lose heart,
Luke 18:1*

*And in that day you will ask Me nothing. Most assuredly,
I say to you, whatever you ask the Father in My name He
will give you.*

*Until now you have asked nothing in My name. Ask, and
you will receive, that your joy may be full.
John 16:23,24*

*Praying always with all prayer and supplication in the
Spirit, being watchful to this end with all perseverance
and supplication for all the saints.
Ephesians 6:18*

Continue earnestly in prayer, being vigilant in it with thanksgiving;
Colossians 4:2

Pray without ceasing,
1 Thessalonians 5:17

Words of encouragement

For a woman in ministry, prayer is very important, and despite your busy schedule, ministry, family responsibilities and the many things competing for your attention, you should make time for prayer.
This is because you're up against far more than you can handle on your own. ***You are not fighting against flesh and blood but against principalities and powers, against the rulers of the darkness of this age, against spiritual hosts of wickedness in the heavenly places. (Ephesians 6:12)***

Prayer is communing with God. It shows your dependence on God - and God is your life! Without Him you are nothing and without Him you can do nothing!

Don't allow life's responsibilities, ministry, and success in ministry, to stop your prayer life. As a matter of fact, you should pray more when you think you're successful or have a lot of responsibilities.

Prayer is essential in ministry, and you should pray long and hard.

Prayer gives you strength, and as such, a prayerless person is a powerless person - very weak. Such a person, even if saved by Jesus, is not safe!

It is also in the place of prayer that you get encouragement, hope, help, divine intervention, and divine direction.

A woman in ministry who does not pray will easily be deceived, discouraged, and defeated by satan.

If you're busy during the day, learn to wake up early in the morning to meet with God in prayer.

You can also pray on your way to work or during lunch time, and when you return home from work.

Prayer works. For example, in *Genesis 32,* Jacob was afraid and he prayed, *"Lord, deliver me, I pray, from the hand of my brother, from the hand of Esau; for I fear him, lest he come and attack me and the mother with the children."*

In his prayer, he reminded God of His promise to him. *"For You said, 'I will surely treat you well, and make your descendants as the sand of the sea, which cannot be numbered for multitude.'" (Genesis 32:11,12)*

Jacob was afraid because of what he had done to Esau, but because he prayed, God touched Esau's heart. In *Genesis 33:4, Esau ran to meet him, and embraced him, and fell on his neck and kissed him, and they wept.*
That's the power of prayer.

No matter where you are or may be going through, pray.

In the Bible, Jonah ran into trouble, but he prayed to the LORD his God from the fish's belly. The Lord heard his prayer, spoke to the fish, and it vomited Jonah onto dry land. *(Jonah 2:1-10 NKJV)*

What a mighty God we serve!

And so, *seek the Lord and His strength; seek His presence continually! (1 Chronicles 16:11 ESV)*

Trust in Him at all times, O people; pour out your heart before Him; God is a refuge for us. (Psalm 62:8 ESV)

Take everything to God in prayer.

This should remind us of this hymn:

What a friend we have in Jesus
All our sins and griefs to bear
What a privilege to carry
Everything to God in prayer
Oh, what peace we often forfeit
Oh, what needless pain we bear
All because we do not carry,
Everything to God in prayer.

Indeed, there's nothing you cannot pray about. You can and should pray about your ministry, finances, needs, family,

marriage, your walk with God, your anxieties, everything –
for we serve a prayer-answering God.

Nothing is too much or too little or too hard to ask God.

***Behold, I am the Lord, the God of all flesh. Is there
anything too hard for Me?
Jeremiah 32:27 NKJV***

The Bible also makes us know that ***the things which are
impossible with men are possible with God. (Luke 18:27)***

Carry everything, without exception, to God in prayer.

God's Words to Women in Ministry

About Rest

And on the seventh day God ended His work which He had done, and He rested on the seventh day from all His work which He had done.
Genesis 2:2 NKJV

Six days you shall do your work, and on the seventh day you shall rest, that your ox and your donkey may rest, and the son of your female servant and the stranger may be refreshed.
Exodus 23:12 NKJV

Six days you shall work, but on the seventh day you shall rest; in plowing time and in harvest you shall rest.
Exodus 34:21 NKJV

I lay down and slept; I awoke, for the Lord sustained me. I will not be afraid of ten thousands of people Who have set themselves against me all around.
Psalms 3:5-6 NKJV

I will both lie down in peace, and sleep; For You alone, O Lord, make me dwell in safety.
Psalms 4:8 NKJV

The Lord is my shepherd; I shall not want. He makes me to lie down in green pastures; He leads me beside the still waters.
Psalms 23:1-2 NKJV

It is useless for you to work so hard from early morning until late at night, anxiously working for food to eat; for God gives rest to his loved ones.
Psalms 127:2 NLT

And suddenly a great tempest arose on the sea, so that the boat was covered with the waves. But He was asleep.
Matthew 8:24 NKJV

Come to Me, all you who labour and are heavy laden, and I will give you rest. Take My yoke upon you and learn from Me, for I am gentle and lowly in heart, and you will find rest for your souls. For My yoke is easy and My burden is light."
Matthew 11:28-30 NKJV

And He said to them, "Come aside by yourselves to a deserted place and rest a while." For there were many coming and going, and they did not even have time to eat. So, they departed to a deserted place in the boat by themselves.
Mark 6:31-32 NKJV

Words of encouragement

When you work a lot and don't rest much, you will eventually become physically, spiritually, and mentally tired.

You have to be careful at such a time because you can easily get discouraged or react to things and people, get angry, and snap. This is because satan usually tries to attack a tired mind with words of discouragement, to deceive the person.

When you find yourself getting upset or feeling discouraged about ministry or life, that may be an indication that you need to rest your body and mind. Take some time off, it's not a sin.

Create a time when you rest. You can't do everything. Do your part in ministry and leave the rest to God. It is His work, and He knows how best to do it.

Let your trust be in God, not in how hard you can work or your abilities.

The Bible reveals that God created the world and rested on the seventh day. He didn't have to rest because He can't be tired. He could have worked but He chose to rest. He knows the importance of rest, and so He gave us an example to follow. It is wise to follow His example. *(Genesis 2:2)*

Rest was also included in the Ten Commandments to emphasise its importance.

Six days you shall labour and do all your work,
but the seventh day is the Sabbath of the Lord your God.
In it you shall do no work: you, nor your son, nor your daughter, nor your male servant, nor your female servant, nor your cattle, nor your stranger who is within your gates.
For in six days the Lord made the heavens and the earth, the sea, and all that is in them, and rested the seventh day. Therefore, the Lord blessed the Sabbath day and hallowed it.
Exodus 20:9-11 NKJV

God gave the children of Israel instructions to rest. They were not to work on the seventh day so that they, and their slaves and animals, could rest and be refreshed.

The children of Israel were to work for six days, they were not to be lazy, and then rest on the seventh day.
Resting does not mean you're lazy. Laziness is too much rest when important things are left undone. Rest on the other hand gets you refreshed.

When you take time to rest, you're not wasting time. Not resting enough can do more harm than good, while resting enough is beneficial.

There's a time to work, and a time to rest even in ministry.

There's a time for everything under heaven. (Ecclesiastes 3:1)

In ***Mark 6:31***, because so many people were coming and going that they did not even have a chance to eat, Jesus said to His disciples, "***Come with Me by yourselves to a quiet place and get some rest.***"

And in ***Matthew 8:24*** the disciples of Jesus found Him sleeping.

You should work hard but don't overwork yourself as it will affect you negatively. Overworking does not translate to breakthrough. Breakthrough and promotion come from God.

So, then it is not of him who wills, nor of him who runs, but of God who shows mercy.
Romans 9:16 NKJV

And according to ***Psalms 127:2 NLT***, it is useless for you to work so hard from early morning until late at night, anxiously working for food to eat; for God gives rest to His loved ones.

You're not blessed by activities but by God. Pray and ask God to bless the work of your hands. Make this one of your prayers.

And let the beauty of the Lord our God be upon us, and establish the work of our hands for us; Yes, establish the work of our hands.
Psalms 90:17 NKJV

Whenever the cares of life want to rob you of peace and rest, remember Jesus' promise.

Come to Me, all you who labour and are heavy laden, and I will give you rest.
Take My yoke upon you and learn from Me, for I am gentle and lowly in heart, and you will find rest for your souls.
For My yoke is easy and My burden is light."
Matthew 11:28-30 NKJV

Resting appropriately prevents burnout. While resting, don't just rest, rest in God. Talk to God and let Him talk to you. Read the Bible and be ministered to. You can also read a good book or go for a walk.

You don't have to do everything, delegate. When you know how to be led by the Holy Spirit, you will know what to say Yes to, when to say no, and you will find rest for your soul.

Rest in God.

God's Words to Women in Ministry

About Sexual temptations

How can a young man keep his way pure? By guarding it according to Your word.
With my whole heart I seek You; let me not wander from Your commandments!
I have stored up Your word in my heart, that I might not sin against You.
Psalms 119:9-11 ESV

And lead us not into temptation, but deliver us from evil.
Matthew 6:13 ESV

Watch and pray that you may not enter into temptation. The spirit indeed is willing, but the flesh is weak.
Matthew 26:41 ESV

... The body is not intended for sexual immorality, but for the Lord, and the Lord is for the body, to save, sanctify, and raise it again because of the sacrifice of the cross.

*Do you not know that your bodies are members of Christ?
Am I therefore to take the members of Christ and make
them part of a prostitute? Certainly not!
Run away from sexual immorality in any form, whether
thought or behavior, whether visual or written.
Every other sin that a man commits is outside the body,
but the one who is sexually immoral sins against his own
body.
Do you not know that your body is a temple of the Holy
Spirit who is within you, whom you have received as a gift
from God, and that you are not your own property?
You were bought with a price you were actually
purchased with the precious blood of Jesus and made His
own.
So then, honor and glorify God with your body.
1 Corinthians 6:13, 15, 18-20 AMP*

*But because of the temptation to sexual immorality, each
man should have his own wife and each woman her own
husband.
1Corinthians 7:2 ESV*

*But if they cannot exercise self-control, they should
marry. For it is better to marry than to burn with passion.
 1Corinthians 7:9 ESV*

*But sexual immorality and all impurity or covetousness
must not even be named among you, as is proper among
saints.
Ephesians 5:3 ESV*

So, flee youthful passions and pursue righteousness, faith, love, and peace, along with those who call on the Lord from a pure heart.
2Timothy 2:22 ESV

Let marriage be held in honor among all, and let the marriage bed be undefiled, for God will judge the sexually immoral and adulterous.
Hebrews 13:4 ESV

Submit yourselves therefore to God. Resist the devil, and he will flee from you.
James 4:7 ESV

Words of encouragement

Don't taint your ministry with sexual scandal.

As I wrote in the novel *The Forever Kind of Love,* Women in ministry could also face this challenge of sexual temptation, but most of the time, pastors, men in ministry, are the ones who are affected.

Quite a number of people have fallen into this trap, but it doesn't have to happen. Don't fall into it.

Any minister, whether male or female, who is not working on his/her marriage and spiritual life could fall into trouble. What satan wants to achieve through this is to strip you of your calling, glory, and family. Run away from every form of sexual immorality like Joseph did, in the Bible!

In the novel *The Forever Kind of Love*, a pastor was warning his ministers about sexual temptation and strange women.

He said, "That is why I'm bringing it up, to caution you and teach you how to resist and overcome this evil. Sadly, quite a number of men of God have sabotaged their ministries by sexual sins. I've had to counsel more than two men of God who fell into adultery ... but may I tell you the truth?

There's really no reason for a man of God to fall into sexual sin or have a sex scandal over his head. It happens because people ignore the words of God and become very careless."

Some of the people nodded in agreement.

The G.O. spoke again. "I have been in the ministry for over thirty two years and I have never had the issue of sex scandal. Never!"

He paused for effect, and then went on. "Am I saying that I'm perfect? No. It has been by God's grace. There are things God has taught me, which I do, and have helped me to stay away from sex scandals. These are the things I want to share with you this morning."

He cleared his throat and continued. "Now, this temptation may not happen in your church. It may be when you're invited to another church to minister."

In the novel, the pastor quoted some Scriptures, said a lot of things and then added, "A foolish one tells himself, 'No one will ever know.' King David in the Bible is an example and he suffered the consequences. Run away from sin. It has the power to keep you longer than you wanted to stay and farther than you wanted to go. It will mess you up. It can cost you everything you've labored for and render you useless."

Whether you're married or single, flee from every appearance of evil, don't compromise God's standard. Be careful where you go and what you do. Be an example of a believer to people around you, and teach them to honor God even with their bodies.

Be sober, be vigilant; because your adversary the devil walks about like a roaring lion, seeking whom he may devour.
Resist him, steadfast in the faith, knowing that the same sufferings are experienced by your brotherhood in the world.
1Peter 5:8-9 NKJV

Finally my brethren, be strong in the Lord and in the power of His might.
Put on the whole armor of God that ye may be able to stand against the wiles of the devil.
For we wrestle not against flesh and blood but against principalities, against powers, against the rulers of the darkness of this world, against spiritual wickedness in high places.
(Ephesians 6:10-12)

Don't taint your ministry with sexual scandal.

God's Words to Women in Ministry

About Testing every spirit

Beware of false prophets, who come to you in sheep's clothing, but inwardly they are ravenous wolves.
Matthew 7:15 NKJV

For false christs and false prophets will rise and show great signs and wonders to deceive, if possible, even the elect.
Matthew 24:24 NKJV

These were more fair-minded than those in Thessalonica, in that they received the word with all readiness, and searched the Scriptures daily to find out whether these things were so.
Acts 17:11 NKJV

to another the working of miracles, to another prophecy, to another discerning of spirits, to another different kinds of tongues, to another the interpretation of tongues.
I Corinthians 12:10 NKJV

For such are false apostles, deceitful workers, transforming themselves into apostles of Christ. And no wonder! For Satan himself transforms himself into an angel of light. Therefore it is no great thing if his ministers also transform themselves into ministers of righteousness, whose end will be according to their works.
II Corinthians 11:13-15 NKJV

Test all things; hold fast what is good. Abstain from every form of evil.
I Thessalonians 5:21-22 NKJV

Beloved, do not believe every spirit, but test the spirits, whether they are of God; because many false prophets have gone out into the world. By this you know the Spirit of God: Every spirit that confesses that Jesus Christ has come in the flesh is of God, and every spirit that does not confess that Jesus Christ has come in the flesh is not of God. And this is the spirit of the Antichrist, which you have heard was coming, and is now already in the world.
I John 4:1-3 NKJV

We are of God. He who knows God hears us; he who is not of God does not hear us. By this we know the spirit of truth and the spirit of error.
I John 4:6 NKJV

Words of encouragement

Do not believe every spirit, but test the spirits, whether they are of God;
because many false prophets have gone out into the world.
I John 4:1 NKJV

The verse above puts the responsibility on you to test every spirit. It's a command. If you believe a false prophet or false prophecy without testing the spirit behind it, it would be your fault.

In my novel *I'll Take You There*, the pastor prayed and then asked the congregation to open their Bibles to *1Thessalonians 5*. He opened his New King James version of the Bible and said, "We'll read from verse 19 to 22. '*Do not quench the Spirit. Do not despise prophecies. Test all things; hold fast what is good. Abstain from every form of evil.*'"

He looked up, asked them to turn their Bibles to *2Peter 2,* and read it from verse 1 to 3.

He went on. "Let's see how The Message Version puts it. '*But there were also lying prophets among the people then, just as there will be lying religious teachers among you. They'll smuggle in destructive divisions, pitting you against each other—biting the hand of the One who gave them a chance to have their lives back! They've put themselves on a fast downhill slide to destruction, but not before they recruit a crowd of mixed-up followers who can't tell right from wrong. They give the way of truth a bad name. They're only out for themselves. They'll say anything, anything, that sounds good to exploit you. They won't, of course, get by with it. They'll come to a bad end, for God has never just stood by and let that kind of thing go on."'*

In his sermon, he said that prophecies should not be despised even though there are lots of fake and demonic prophets and pastors. He added that people should believe in the supernatural manifestations of God and prophecies, but should not accept every prophecy or everyone who claims to be a prophet.

He went on. "Scriptures warn that false prophets will arise to deceive many, including Christians who are not well-grounded in the word of God. These false prophets and false pastors are all over the place. You can meet them in a store or market, on the road … anywhere."

He said that false prophets operate by a lying spirit, familiar spirits, and other demonic spirits.

"Their prophecies may even be correct, but accepting them will take your eyes off God." He warned. "If they come to you to give you some words, tell them no, God can't bypass

your pastor to talk to them about you. You can say this if your pastor is genuinely of God."

Spirits should be tested because satan can counterfeit the works of God.

For false christs and false prophets will rise and show great signs and wonders to deceive, if possible, even the elect. See, I have told you beforehand.
Matthew 24:24-25 NKJV

Counterfeit is to make a copy of something with the intent to deceive people.

And no wonder, for even satan disguises himself as an angel of light.
2 Corinthians 11:14 ESV

Jesus said by their fruits you shall know them! This is because these false prophets may be able to fake the works of God, but they can't live like a true servant of God, in righteousness.

A good tree cannot bear bad fruit, nor can a bad tree bear good fruit.

Therefore by their fruits you will know them.
Matthew 7:15, 18, 20 NKJV

Do not believe every spirit, but test the spirits, whether they are of God.

God's Words to Women in Ministry

When having financial issues

The Lord will open to you His good treasure, the heavens, to give the rain to your land in its season, and to bless all the work of your hand. You shall lend to many nations, but you shall not borrow.
And the Lord will make you the head and not the tail; you shall be above only, and not be beneath, if you heed the commandments of the Lord your God, which I command you today, and are careful to observe them.
Deuteronomy 28:12-13 NKJV

Let them shout for joy and be glad, Who favour my righteous cause; And let them say continually, "Let the Lord be magnified, Who has pleasure in the prosperity of His servant."
Psalms 35:27 NKJV

In all labor there is profit, But idle chatter leads only to poverty.
Proverbs 14:23 NKJV

The crown of the wise is their riches, But the foolishness of fools is folly.
Proverbs 14:24 NKJV

The plans of the diligent lead surely to plenty, But those of everyone who is hasty, surely to poverty.
Proverbs 21:5 NKJV

The wise have wealth and luxury, but fools spend whatever they get.
Proverbs 21:20 NLT

The rich rules over the poor, and the borrower is servant to the lender.
Proverbs 22:7 NKJV

Prepare your outside work, Make it fit for yourself in the field; And afterward build your house.
Proverbs 24:27 NKJV

For which of you, intending to build a tower, does not sit down first and count the cost, whether he has enough to finish it, lest, after he has laid the foundation, and is not able to finish, all who see it begin to mock him, saying, 'This man began to build and was not able to finish'?
Luke 14:28-30 NKJV

If any of you lacks wisdom, let him ask of God, who gives to all liberally and without reproach, and it will be given to him.
James 1:5 NKJV

Words of encouragement

Several Scriptures in the Bible such as *Psalms 35:27* make it clear that God has pleasure in the prosperity of His ministers.

The Bible also reveals that the earth is the Lord's and the fullness thereof, and that gold and silver belong to Him. But sometimes, God's children lack, they are in want, and some are neck deep in debt. This is not God's will for you.

In *2Kings*, a widow had financial issues. She was given certain instructions which she obeyed, and God delivered her and her children from the financial mess. God wants to deliver you too.

No matter how you got into this financial challenge, God's will is that you come out of the challenge. He wants you to have financial freedom, be able to meet your needs, do your ministry, honour Him with your wealth, and give to the less privileged.

When people are in debt, they are tempted to borrow more money, but that is not the solution.

Getting out of financial challenges

1)To get out of the tight situation, the first thing is to know that God wants you to prosper. Lack does not glorify God. He wants to provide for you. Another thing to know is that you can actually come out and be absolutely debt free, if you do what God is leading you to do.

2)The next thing is to pray. Present your case, and needs before God. Also ask Him for wisdom and help, to know how to handle your finances the right way. While you're at it, ask for forgiveness for however you contributed to the trouble.

3)Check yourself, your assets, your liabilities, and your spending habits. Do you pay your tithe and give offerings? How much comes in and how much do you spend? What do you own, and owe?

"Will a man rob God? Yet you have robbed Me! But you say, 'In what way have we robbed You?' In tithes and offerings.
You are cursed with a curse, For you have robbed Me, Even this whole nation.
Bring all the tithes into the storehouse, That there may be food in My house, And try Me now in this," Says the Lord of hosts, "If I will not open for you the windows of heaven And pour out for you such blessing That there will not be room enough to receive it.
"And I will rebuke the devourer for your sakes, So that he will not destroy the fruit of your ground, Nor shall the

vine fail to bear fruit for you in the field," Says the Lord of hosts;
"And all nations will call you blessed, For you will be a delightful land," Says the Lord of hosts.
Malachi 3:8-12 NKJV

4)Correct yourself. Make up your mind to begin to pay tithe and give offerings.

Honour the Lord with your possessions, and with the firstfruits of all your increase.
Proverbs 3:9

5)Correct your spending habits. Cut off unnecessary expenses, refrain from buying things you don't need, and see where you can save some money. Be content with what you have.

6)If you're in debts, don't borrow more money. Begin to think of how you can repay it. If necessary, talk to your creditors and work out a repayment plan.

7)Prayerfully think of other streams of income, what can be done to earn additional income. Pray and if you feel led by God, get a job or start a business that will not hinder your ministry or affect your family negatively.

In the Bible, some churches supported Apostle Paul, but he also had another source of income – he was a tent maker.

He told the Corinthians, *"And we labour, working with our own hands. ..." (I Corinthians 4:12 NKJV)*

After these things Paul departed from Athens and went to Corinth.
And he found a certain Jew named Aquila, born in Pontus, who had recently come from Italy with his wife Priscilla (because Claudius had commanded all the Jews to depart from Rome); and he came to them.
So, because he was of the same trade, he stayed with them and worked; for by occupation they were tentmakers.
And he reasoned in the synagogue every Sabbath, and persuaded both Jews and Greeks.
Acts 18:1-4 NKJV

And so, Paul worked with the couple, and did his ministry, teaching in the synagogue every Sabbath.

In my novel **With This Ring**, Pastor Femi had a business and put someone in charge.

Mondays and Saturdays were his two off-duty days, and he only went to church on those days if there was a special program or something he had to do. He usually spent Mondays at the small office he rented for his transport business, to see Dayo, the man he employed to monitor the business.

When Femi relocated to Nigeria, he registered and started the business of providing bus services to young schools that could not afford to buy their own buses. He bought some buses, employed drivers, and now had a number of schools using the service. He also had two cabs, and with Dayo, an honest male graduate as the manager, Femi didn't have any problem.

Be disciplined, commit yourself to these things, and keep praying.

Involve God in all that you do.

About the author

Taiwo Iredele Odubiyi is a Pastor and the Executive President of TenderHearts Family Support Initiative, a Non-Governmental Organization, and Pastor Taiwo Odubiyi Ministries. She has a deep and strong passion for relationships and expresses this in ministries - nationally and internationally- to children, teenagers, singles, women and couples. She reaches out to these groups through counselling, seminars and programs such as Teenslink, Singleslink, Coupleslink, and Woman to Woman.

Married and blessed with children, she is the regular host of the TV and Radio program - It's all about you!

I love hearing from the readers of my books. If this book has blessed you, please send your comments to:

WhatsApp: +1-410 8187482
Website: www.pastortaiwoodubiyi.org
Facebook: Pastor Mrs. Taiwo Odubiyi
        Pastor Taiwo Iredele Odubiyi's novels & books
Twitter: @pastortaiwoodub
Instagram: @pastortaiwoiredeleodubiyi

If you have friends and loved ones, then you do have people you should bless with copies of these very interesting and life-changing novels and books!

www.ingramcontent.com/pod-product-compliance
Lightning Source LLC
Chambersburg PA
CBHW051442130726
47987CB00005B/2161